BLOOM'S ReViews

COMPREHENSIVE | RESEARCH & STUDY GUIDES

Richard Wright's
Native Son

Edited & with
an Introduction
by Harold Bloom

3 5 7 9 8 6 4 2

The Chelsea House World Wide Web site address is
http://www.chelseahouse.com

Library of Congress Cataloging-in-Publication Data

Bloom, Harold.
Richard Wright's Native Son / Harold Bloom, editor.
p. cm. — (Bloom's Reviews)
Includes bibliographical references and index.
Summary: Includes a brief biography of the author, thematic and structural analysis of the work, critical views, and an index of themes and ideas.
ISBN 0-7910-4068-2 (hc)   ISBN 0-7910-4139-5 (pb)
1. Wright, Richard, 1908-1960. Native Son. 2. Afro-Americans in litera-
ture. [1. Wright, Richard, 1908-1960. Native Son. 2. American litera-
ture.— History and criticism.] I. Bloom, Harold. II. Series.
PS3545.R815N344 1995
813'.52—dc20
95-45097
CIP
AC

Chelsea House Publishers
1974 Sproul Road, Suite 400
P.O. Box 914
Broomall, PA 19008-0914

Contents

Editor's Note

My Introduction argues that the influence of Dreiser upon Richard Wright was more fecund than that of Dostoevsky, in determining the nature of Bigger Thomas. Critical Views commence with Malcolm Cowley, who prophesied that the novel would admonish white America. The African-American novelist James Baldwin judges Bigger to be a true descendant of Uncle Tom in Harriet Beecher Stowe's novel, because Bigger has internalized white racist views of blacks.

Narrative force is praised by Robert Bone as one of *Native Son's* excellences, while Irving Howe regards the novel as being equally uncomfortable reading for both whites and blacks. The great African-American novelist Ralph Ellison denies any continuity between Wright's work and his own, while expressing a personal admiration for the pioneer modern black writer.

Dan McCall examines the relation between Wright and Bigger, while Edward Margolies finds the pattern of Wright's politics in the book, and Roger Rosenblatt concludes that whiteness, for Bigger and Richard Wright alike, is the emblem of nothingness, a force but not a form.

The novel is defended against accusations of black racism by Dorothy S. Redden, but then is chastised by Sherley Anne Williams for its inadequate representations of black women. Narrative technique is examined by A. Robert Lee, after which Judith Giblin Brazinsky studies differences between the novel and its dramatic version by Wright and Paul Green.

Speechlessness as Bigger's mode is expounded by Louis Tremaine, while Robert James Butler considers Bigger's dual attitude towards Mary. Joyce Ann Joyce centers upon Bigger's Communist defense lawyer, after which Bigger's painful difficulties in expressing himself are analyzed by Laura E. Tanner. Misogyny, common alas both to Bigger and to Wright, is examined by Alan W. France, while the less mournful question of surrealism in the book is taken up by Eugene E. Miller. Existentialism, a later French literary fashion, is found in the novel by Jean-Francois Gounard, after which James Campbell concludes by considering the general relationship between the Paris of Sartre and Richard Wright.

Introduction

HAROLD BLOOM

Symbolic murders are unacceptable in life, and can be a little hard to take in literature. Before writing *Native Son,* Richard Wright had published a collection of short stories, *Uncle Tom's Children,* which can be regarded as little else but symbolic murders, of whites by blacks, with consequent retributions. Criminal rebellion can be approved as rebellion, when the historical injustices are overwhelming, as they have been and still are for many African Americans. Individual murder is a somewhat different matter, which is one of the reasons why *Native Son* remains so profoundly painful a book. In an earlier introduction to it, I quoted John M. Reilly, a critical follower of Wright, who, in an afterword to an edition of *Native Son,* told us that "the description of Mary's murder makes clear that the white world is the cause of the violent desires and reactions" that motivated Bigger Thomas to murder Mary Dalton. I remarked in rejoinder, that Wright's novelistic description was quite sufficient to make clear that Bigger Thomas's desires and reactions are somewhat overdetermined, but that he is neither a replicant nor a psychopathic child. He is therefore culpable, if he is a representation of a person and not a mere ideogram.

Eight years of some rather nasty responses to my remarks have not changed my judgment, since those responses detract from the stature of Wright's novel as a novel, rather than a mere social document. Bigger, a Native Son, remains an individual; he suffers and dies as an individual, and he murders as an individual. Wright's narrative strength depends upon Bigger's personal intensity and detailed, naturalistic vividness. The book asks us to comprehend Bigger's hatreds, but surely not to approve of them. As Dan McCall wrote:

> We do not "sympathize" with Bigger. We *feel with* him, perhaps, but we do it in a special way. When Frantz Fanon speaks of violence, and the necessity for it, he addresses himself to a revolutionary social situation. "Violence" is impelled by consciousness. . . . Violence is not a helpless reflex, a gross futility, an insane outburst. . . . But the violent blood baths of Bigger Thomas are at the mercy of the system which engendered them.

Empathy, like sympathy, does not seem the accurate response to Wright's Bigger. He murders Mary because he is driven by hatred of all whites; he murders his own girlfriend, Bessie, who is black, in order to free himself from a filial relationship to her. Like Dostoevsky's Raskolnikov in *Crime and Punishment,* Bigger seeks freedom through the murder of Bessie, thus affirming his own will, yet that seems to me more Richard Wright than Bigger Thomas. The nihilistic aspect of *Native Son* is less persuasive than its Dreiserian, naturalistic element, where Bigger is more at home. He is too desperately blinded by his own hatred and his own dependencies to be judged a nihilist; perhaps more education might have enabled him to quest after such an illusion, or given him some inner shield against the self-destructiveness of his own ferocity.

Abdul R. Jan Mohamed, writing on what he calls the "psychopolitical function of death" in Richard Wright's work, asks us to see that violent death, particularly in *Native Son,* serves as a means of escape from "social death," the death-in-life of the slave, or ex-slave, or descendant of a slave still not emancipated by a repressive society. "Psychopolitics" is for me a difficult notion, yet the idea that powerlessness is a "social death" has undoubted force, and does provide a somewhat precarious illumination for Wright's most famous book (his autobiography, *Black Boy,* seems to me a larger aesthetic achievement). Theodore Dreiser, Wright's authentic precursor, is similarly illuminated by the idea, and the protagonists of *An American Tragedy* and *Sister Carrie* are after all not slaves or ex-slaves. Dreiser has terrible opacities, but his best novels are redeemed by a massive pathos. *Black Boy* tells us that Wright read Dreiser's *Sister Carrie* and *Jennie Gerhardt,* and they revived in him a vivid sense of his own mother's suffering. Perhaps *Native Son,* on Marxist grounds, refused to give us such a sense of Bigger Thomas's suffering. Bigger is meant to terrify us, and he does, but Wright has the skill to show us that all too frequently Bigger acts out of intense fear, a realistic terror of the world. Fanon argues that Bigger kills only as a response to the world's expectation that he must kill or die. It is difficult to accept such an argument, in a novel, where almost anything is possible. Richard Wright accepted the aesthetic risk of making Bigger Thomas inarticulate. The risk may have been too great; Bigger goes to his execution in the self-conviction that he is neither better nor worse than most men. A sociopath, to persuade us of that, must be granted eloquence, a certain style of near madness. Wright needed to make his book too harsh for us; we are still so guilty a society that the more humane among us, black and white, feel that we must accept Wright's harshness. If a better time—now nowhere apparent—ever comes in relations between the races in our country, then *Native Son* may yield place among Wright's books to the more poignant and personal *Black Boy.* ❖

Biography of Richard Wright

Richard Nathaniel Wright was born on September 4, 1908, near Natchez, Mississippi, to a schoolteacher mother and an illiterate sharecropper father. His father abandoned the family when Wright was very young, and he was raised by his maternal grandmother. After ninth grade, he dropped out of school and moved to Memphis, then to Chicago and New York. He educated himself and was particularly interested in literature, sociology, and psychology. In 1932 he joined the Communist party, and his literary career was encouraged by the communist-affiliated John Reed Club. Much of his early writing appeared in leftist publications. He worked for the Federal Negro Theatre Project and the Federal Writers' Project; while associated with these organizations he published *12 Million Black Voices* (1941), a Marxist analysis of the American class struggle. He was Harlem editor for the *Daily Worker* in New York. In 1938 he married Rose Dhima Meadman; they were later divorced, and Wright married Ellen Poplar, with whom he had two children. From 1947 until his death he lived in Paris.

Wright first came to the attention of the American reading public with the publication of *Uncle Tom's Children: Four Novellas* in 1938; the stories concern the struggles to maturity of oppressed black women and men. An augmented edition including the novelette "Bright and Morning Star" appeared in 1940. Wright's second book, *Native Son* (1940), was his major critical and popular breakthrough and remains one of the most influential American novels of the twentieth century. It concerns the life and destruction of Bigger Thomas, a poor black youth from the slums of Chicago. Wright's evocative portrayal of a life of fear and enslavement struck a powerful chord with his readership, despite some critics' complaints that the latter third of the book is expository and slow moving.

Though none of Wright's subsequent books had the immediate impact of *Native Son,* he was admired as a solid stylist and spokesman for the poor and oppressed. His later novels are *The Outsider* (1953), *Savage Holiday* (1954), *The Long Dream*

(1958), and *Lawd Today* (1963). *Eight Men,* a collection of stories, was published posthumously in 1961. His autobiography, *Black Boy: A Record of Childhood and Youth* (1945), and his sociological studies, including *Black Power: A Record of Reactions in a Land of Pathos* (1954), *The Color Curtain: A Report on the Bandung Conference* (1956; originally published in French in 1955), *Pagan Spain* (1956), and *White Man, Listen!* (1957), were also widely read and admired. Wright died on November 28, 1960. Another autobiography, *American Hunger,* was published in 1977; *Richard Wright Reader,* edited by Ellen Wright and Michel Fabre, was published in 1978. ❖

Thematic and Structural Analysis

Book one, "Fear," begins with the Thomas family waking up in their home. The images that dominate the opening are of cramped and crowded conditions. The family of four—the mother, sister Vera, brother Buddy, and Bigger—share a tiny one-room apartment on the South Side of Chicago that lacks all privacy: The boys must turn their heads when the mother and daughter change clothes, as they do in turn for the boys. This "conspiracy against shame" introduces a theme of self-consciousness that continues throughout the novel; there is almost immediately a sense of being watched by others.

The family's morning routine is interrupted by the sound of a rat. It is a familiar situation: The women are frantic; the boys, initially, are motionless. But Bigger, the elder of the two sons (later identified as twenty years old), traps and kills the rat in a scene that prefigures the violent episodes later in the novel. In the nasty battle, the rat, which is "over a foot long," fearful, and defiant, rips a three-inch hole in Bigger's pant-leg. After he kills the rat, Bigger teases his sister by dangling it in front of her and frightening her so much that she faints. Bigger's mother scolds him with regret: "[S]ometimes I wonder why I birthed you."

Bigger's mother reminds him that he has a job interview that afternoon, which the relief office has arranged; in order for the Thomases to continue to be eligible for assistance, he must take the position. Bigger resents both the interview and the job, as well as the nagging of his mother.

Bigger spends the day hanging around his neighborhood. At the pool hall he meets up with his friends, Gus, G.H., and Jack, with whom he discusses their plan to rob Blum's Deli that afternoon. Despite it being a quick and easy job, the crime is riskier than others they have committed because it will be their first against a white. Their apprehension about the robbery reflects their greater fear of whites and their realization that the law is harder on blacks who commit crimes against whites.

The young men's consciousness of racial difference emerges when they engage in a game of "playing white"—impersonating military figures and the millionaire banker J.P. Morgan. The seemingly lighthearted game gives way to a conversation about the limits that whites have imposed on them, with Bigger commenting, "Half the time I feel like I'm on the outside of the world peeping through a knot-hole in the fence. . . ." When Bigger asks Gus if he knows where the "white folks" live, Gus replies predictably: across the boundary that marks the Black Belt from other areas of the city. But Bigger corrects him by pointing to his own body, saying, "Right down here in my stomach." The comment underscores the pervasive whiteness that invades them, marking every aspect of their lives.

After a scuffle with Gus, Bigger goes to the movies with Jack, and the two watch a double feature: *The Gay Woman* and *Trader Horn*. The first movie is a parodically conventional if not exaggerated film about a beautiful and wealthy white married woman who has an adulterous affair. At a key moment, the woman's lover saves a crowd from a bomb thrown by a Communist. But the story is ultimately resolved by the woman's return to her capitalist husband. Bigger and Jack are amused and enchanted by the film's representation of a life of mythic pleasure and drama that is inaccessible to them. The second feature is a film of African scenes that Bigger replaces with "images in his own mind of white men and women." The double billing of the two films juxtaposes white and black realities and expectations. This opposition between black and white, as well as between rich and poor, recurs throughout the novel, both thematically and within Bigger's consciousness.

(Wright wrote this scene to replace the much rawer one included in his original version of the novel, in which the two friends masturbate and then watch a newsreel of "the daughters of the rich taking sunbaths in the sands of Florida," which shows Mary Dalton, the daughter of the man with whom Bigger has an interview, embracing her Communist boyfriend, whom her parents have denounced.)

The young men eventually meet again in Doc's pool hall at the appointed time. Bigger is anxious about the robbery, becoming even more nervous because Gus, whom he accuses of being a coward, is late. When Gus does appear, Bigger uses his lateness as an excuse to start a fight with him and not go ahead with the job. Bigger leaves the pool hall, feeling "an overwhelming desire to be alone," and goes home before his 5:30 job interview.

Later, as he heads over to the Dalton home, he is conscious of crossing into the white neighborhood. When he arrives at the house, a strange woman (whom Bigger later learns is the blind Mrs. Dalton) lets him in. He then meets Mr. Dalton, who asks Bigger about his education, work experience, and living situation, as well as why he was sent to reform school, embarrassing Bigger. But Mr. Dalton offers him the job as driver for which the pay is twenty-five dollars a week (five dollars more than it "calls for") and includes room, board, and clothing.

During the interview with Mr. Dalton, Mary, the Daltons' daughter, enters. She immediately asks Bigger if he belongs to a union, and when he responds negatively, she asks, "And why not?" The scene reflects a somewhat humorous tension between Mary and her father, whom she jokingly calls "Mr. Capitalist." But Bigger perceives Mary as a dangerous troublemaker. Mr. Dalton explains to Bigger that he is hiring him because he is a supporter of the National Association for the Advancement of Colored People (NAACP); Bigger does not know what this is.

Mr. Dalton introduces Bigger to Peggy, the cook, who tells him that he is also responsible for maintaining the furnace. Peggy, an Irish immigrant, analogizes the experience of the Irish at the hands of the British to the experience of "colored folks" in the United States. She also describes the previous person in Bigger's position: a man named Green who held the job for ten years; who, with Mr. Dalton's assistance, attended school; and who now works for the government. But Bigger privately rejects the idea of Green as a role model. After instructing Bigger how to look after the furnace, Peggy shows him to his room above the kitchen.

While alone in his room, Bigger reflects on his new life and its possibilities. But when he returns to the kitchen to get a glass of water, he is interrupted by Mrs. Dalton, an arresting figure of whiteness, whom he finds perplexing; because of her blindness he feels that she is someone he can "scarcely see." He also sees her as one who would judge him "harshly but kindly."

Bigger's first task is to drive Mary to university that evening. But Mary tells him to drive her to the Loop instead, where they pick up Jan Erlone, a young white man and a Communist. Despite, or perhaps because of, their overly familiar behavior and seemingly progressive politics, Mary and Jan cause Bigger to be "conscious of his black skin"; he feels "naked, transparent," in their presence.

Jan takes over driving the car, with Bigger sitting between him and Mary in the front seat. Mary asks Bigger to take them to a place "where colored people eat," and Bigger suggests Ernie's Kitchen Shack. When they arrive at the restaurant, Mary and Jan expect Bigger to eat with them, and although Bigger first refuses, he acquiesces because of Mary's crying. Bigger notices Bessie, his girlfriend, and is embarrassed to be seen with the whites. As Mary, Jan, and Bigger eat fried chicken and drink beer, Bigger, self-conscious of his movements, feels angry and trapped. Before they leave, they order a bottle of rum.

Mary tells Bigger that she is going to Detroit the next day and that he should deliver her trunk to the railroad station in the morning, thus reestablishing Bigger's social role as a worker. Bigger drives around Washington Park while Mary and Jan sit together in the back seat, fooling around and drinking the rum, which they share with Bigger. They discuss Communism and the necessity of mobilizing the "negroes" and ask Bigger to sing spirituals. After they drop off Jan, Mary moves up to the front seat next to Bigger. She is drunk, flirtatious, and aggressive.

When they arrive at the Dalton house, Bigger must help Mary inside and carry her upstairs. He cannot find her room because she is too drunk to respond to his questions, and he is terrified of walking into the Daltons' bedroom with Mary in his arms. When he finds her room, he puts her in bed and becomes fascinated by the physical closeness. He begins touching and caressing her but is interrupted when Mrs. Dalton enters the room. Bigger, seized with panic, covers Mary's face with a pillow. Mrs. Dalton continues to call to Mary, and from the smell of liquor she realizes that Mary is drunk. Finally, Mrs. Dalton leaves.

When Bigger lifts the pillow, Mary is silent and unconscious, and Bigger realizes that he has suffocated her. In his panic, he tries to dispose of her body, which he places in the trunk and carries to the basement. He tries to burn Mary's body in the furnace, placing all of her up to her shoulders into the fire. The rest will not fit, so in a gruesome scene, Bigger hacks at Mary's head with his knife and then finally grabs a hatchet, which he uses to slice off her head in a single blow, carefully placing newspaper underneath her body to soak up the blood. He then pushes the body, head, and hatchet into the furnace and covers them with coal so they will burn. He decides to tell the Daltons that after he took Mary's trunk to the basement, he left her in the car with Jan. The book ends with Bigger's return to his family's apartment.

Book two, "Flight," plots Bigger's efforts to hide the crime, to avoid becoming a suspect, and, ultimately, to escape the police. Unlike in the first book, Bigger now exhibits a greater sense of independence and agency, as if the crime has liberated him. The themes that run through the second book are Bigger's ability to see—as opposed to being seen—as well as his awareness of the "blindness" of those around him. The image dominating the second book is one of pervasive whiteness: This part of the novel opens with daylight and a snowfall that gradually escalates into a blizzard.

Bigger, back at his family's apartment, awakens in the bed that he shares with Buddy. Only when Bigger is fully awake does he begin to remember the crime he committed just hours before. He finds Mary's purse atop his trousers, and in his pockets he discovers the Communist pamphlets that Jan had given him. He disposes of the purse and plans to leave the pamphlets in his room at the Dalton house to plant suspicion of Jan. There is also much arguing in the opening to the second book: Bigger angrily contradicts his mother and insists that he returned at two o'clock; Vera accuses him of "looking under" her dress.

After Bigger leaves the apartment, he is not afraid but "eager" and "excited." He has a daydream of blacks, through their own leadership, conquering their oppressors and ascending to power, which suggests a resistance to the "help" offered to blacks by both the Daltons and Communist figures such as Jan. In Bigger's thoughts, justice for blacks will come only through their own efforts. And Bigger believes that with the violence he has committed, "his whole life [is] caught up in a supreme and a meaningful act."

He eventually returns to the Dalton house, where he stokes the furnace, checks that Mary's body is burning, and then takes her trunk to the railroad station. Upon his return, he over-hears the conversation between Peggy and Mrs. Dalton from his room above the kitchen. They worry about Mary's where-abouts, and Bigger begins to feel fear.

Mrs. Dalton comes to his room to ask him about Mary and what happened the night before. Bigger is aware that "a cer-tain element of shame would keep Mrs. Dalton from asking him too much." He anticipates Mrs. Dalton's reserve and plays on it to his advantage in concealing his crime. Bigger considers the series of binary oppositions that inform his world: white/black, rich/poor, boss/worker, and old/young.

He then leaves to visit Bessie, who immediately confronts him about his "white friends" from the previous night and asks him about the money he is carrying (which he took from Mary's purse before disposing of it). Although Bessie seems to suspect that Bigger has done something terribly wrong, he does not confide in her. Then Bessie mentions the Leopold and Loeb case, which, according to her, took place nearby. The case, in which two sons of wealthy businessmen killed a fourteen-year-old boy, hid the body, and sent a ransom note to the dead boy's father, gives Bigger the idea of making the crime seem a kidnapping to extort ransom money from the Daltons. Bigger thinks that "maybe he could use" Bessie; he ponders her life, her limitations, and her work as a domestic servant for whites. In his thoughts, he separates Bessie into two distinct beings: the Bessie of her body, whom he uses for plea-sure, and the Bessie of her face, who confronts him unpleas-antly with questions. His desire is to "blot out" the Bessie of the face, so that what is left is the Bessie of the body that he "[wants] badly."

They go to the Paris Grill, where Bigger tells Bessie that Mary and Jan have eloped and suggests writing a ransom note to play on her parents' fears of kidnapping. He convinces Bessie to be his accomplice. Bigger has "new fears," but they are allayed by "new feelings." He is more alive, and "[f]or the first time in his life he [moves] consciously between two sharply different poles . . . away from the threatening penalty of death . . . toward the sense of fullness he [has] so often but inadequately felt in magazines and movies."

Leaving Bessie, he returns to the Dalton house, where he is instructed by Mrs. Dalton to retrieve the trunk from the station. The trunk was not picked up; the Daltons have received a wire from Detroit saying that Mary did not arrive. After Bigger returns, he is confronted by Mr. Dalton and a private investigator, Britten, who, when they open the trunk and discover that it is only half-packed, ask Bigger to recount the past night's events. Britten is particularly aggressive and suspects Bigger of being a Communist. He pulls out the Communist pamphlets he has found in Bigger's room and questions Bigger about them. Bigger, with Mr. Dalton's support, convinces Britten that he is not a Communist, and Bigger goes back to his room, where he is able to hear the conversation between Britten and Mr. Dalton. In the second book, Bigger is frequently in a position of listening and overhearing.

Jan eventually arrives and is questioned by Britten and Mr. Dalton. When Bigger tells the men that Jan brought Mary home the night before, Jan assumes that Bigger has been forced to lie. Jan denies coming to the Dalton home but confesses to spending the evening with Mary and Bigger. Dalton tries to bribe Jan to learn about Mary's whereabouts, but Jan is insulted by this action and leaves.

Later, when Bigger goes out, Jan confronts him, accusing him of lying. Jan seems convinced that Bigger is merely acting on the wishes of the Daltons. Bigger repeats again and again, "Leave me alone!" until finally he threatens Jan with his gun. Jan leaves, and Bigger goes to a drugstore and buys an envelope, paper, and pencil in order to compose the ransom note.

Bigger notices a sign for the South Side Real Estate Company, which causes him to think of the property that Mr. Dalton owns and the segregation and poverty that he imposes upon Chicago's blacks, despite his philanthropy, by enforcing the boundaries of the Black Belt through real estate. Mr. Dalton is the landlord of Bigger's family: It is to him, this millionaire and philanthropist, that they pay eight dollars a week for "one rat-infested room."

Returning to Bessie's apartment, Bigger writes the ransom note, into which he puts considerable effort. He prints with his left hand although he is right-handed, and he stops himself from writing "I," instead writing "we." The gesture seems logical: He tries to include Bessie as an accomplice in this scheme and hopes to confuse the investigators by suggesting that more than one person is involved. But this act also signifies that Bigger is not acting alone; he still cannot fully articulate his independent agency. He signs the note "*Red*" and draws a hammer and sickle.

Bessie confronts Bigger with her suspicion that he has killed Mary. When he confesses, she grows hysterical; to quiet her, Bigger first says that she is now implicated in the crime and then threatens to kill her. He then takes Bessie to the empty building where she will wait for the ransom to be delivered the next night. Then he leaves her and returns to the Dalton house, where he slips the note under the front door. The scene is marked with self-consciousness, for this action reminds Bigger of his inability to use the front entrance.

Bigger then enters the house through the back and goes to the basement to fuel the furnace and check on Mary's body. Realizing his hunger, he goes upstairs into the kitchen, where Peggy comes in and heats up his dinner. Peggy has retrieved the note, which she gives to Mr. Dalton.

After Mr. Dalton reads the note, he calls Britten back to the house. Soon reporters arrive, and Bigger is called downstairs to the basement, where they are gathered around the furnace. The story of Mary's disappearance has been leaked to the press by Jan, who, on orders from Mr. Dalton, has been picked up by the police and held for questioning. At first, Mr. Dalton remains upstairs while Britten fields the questions. Bigger learns that Mr. Dalton has not gone to the police but intends to pay the ransom to get Mary back safely. Bigger is also questioned. He words his answers about Jan's Communist beliefs carefully, because "he knew the things white folks hated to hear Negroes ask for; and he knew that these were the things the Reds were asking for." Then Mr. Dalton, soon followed by Mrs. Dalton, comes down to the basement to speak to the press.

Mr. Dalton says he has requested Jan's release and will not press charges against him. He asks the press to carry the story so that the kidnappers will know that the Daltons will comply with their demands. We learn also that Jan, in protest, has refused to leave jail and claims to have an alibi. He swears that the family knows where Mary is and "this thing is a stunt to raise a cry against the Reds." The reporters remain and question Bigger further. Then Britten pulls out the Communist pamphlets given to Bigger by Jan.

Peggy brings hot coffee down to the men and instructs Bigger to clean out the ashes and "make a better fire." Bigger tries to shift the ashes to allow more air in without having to shovel out the ashes and thus reveal Mary's charred remains. When smoke begins to fill the basement, one of the men takes the shovel from Bigger and cleans out the ashes, dumping them on the floor. Then Bigger watches as the man sifts through the ashes and gradually discovers pieces of white bone and an earring.

With this discovery, a feeling returns to Bigger that "he [is] black and [has] done wrong." And with this comes the return of self-consciousness: He is being watched by white men. Bigger leaves, tiptoeing up the stairs to his room, where he locks the door behind him, crawls out the window, and jumps to the ground.

The running away is "familiar"; Bigger reflects that he has "always felt outside the white world, and now it [is] true." He again goes to Bessie's, where he finds her half-asleep and tells her how he killed Mary. Bessie plants the idea that Bigger will be accused of raping Mary as well.

In the scenes that unfold, Bigger begins to think of Bessie as a "dangerous burden." She begs to leave with him but then reconsiders: "What's the use of running? They'll catch us anywhere." The two go into an abandoned building, where Bigger begins to make sexual advances toward Bessie. She resists, and he rapes her. Bessie falls asleep, and Bigger lies awake, regretting telling her that he murdered Mary. He again feels the burden of Bessie: "[I]t was his life against hers." Fearing that she will turn him in, he beats Bessie to death with a brick and pushes her body into an air shaft, realizing regretfully that the money from Mary's purse is in her pocket.

Bigger contemplates the murders he has committed: "In all of his life these two murders were the most meaningful things that had ever happened to him. He was living truly and deeply. . . . never had his will been so free. . . ." Having achieved a higher level of consciousness after the crimes, Bigger realizes that, as a black man, "never [have] the two worlds of thought and feeling, will and mind, aspiration and satisfaction, been together, never [has] he felt a sense of wholeness." Only violence and hate have resolved his inner conflict and made him "capable of action." What he wants is "to merge himself with others and be a part of this world . . . to be allowed a chance to live like others, even though he [is] black."

The image of the blizzard dominates the rest of the second book. The city is slowed, almost stopped, by the snowstorm. The whiteness and coldness of the snow and ice are inescapable, pursuing Bigger at every turn.

Bigger steals a newspaper and learns that he is considered the perpetrator of a "sex crime" and that the story has inspired a rash of crimes against blacks in the city. The police suspect Jan Erlone as well, because "the plan of the murder and kidnaping was too elaborate to be the work of a Negro mind." Scores of police and vigilantes sweep over the city in search of Bigger, but the newspapers keep him informed of the pattern and range of the sweep, publishing a map whose shaded portions indicate the areas already searched. To remain safe, Bigger must continue to hide in an area in "the white portion" of the map. There is a peculiar liveliness to these passages: It is as if Bigger is pursued not simply by the police but by the headlines themselves and the exaggerated stories of the tabloids.

Bigger climbs to the roof of an abandoned building, from which he watches a black family through a window of their small apartment. Three children are sitting on a bed watching a man and woman in the same room have sex. The scene is "familiar" to Bigger.

Bigger continues his flight from the law, realizing that the police are in constant pursuit of him and that he will soon be caught. Still, he does not give up but climbs to the rooftops. The closing scenes in book two describe the attempts by the police to capture Bigger. Finally, overcome with the cold and ice, exhausted and hungry, he lets himself be caught.

Book three, "Fate," opens with a somewhat melancholic meditation on time; Bigger is in jail awaiting trial, and for him there is no distinction between day and night, an interesting conversion of the earlier polarities. This book presents a striking contrast to the others; it is less concerned with activity and instead is more ruminative.

Bigger is now passive and inattentive—"in the grip of a deep physiological resolution not to react to anything," determined to "[turn] away from his life." He is physically constrained, even shackled while moving. He is taken to the Cook County Morgue and in a dreamlike passage is presented, in shackles, to the Daltons and Jan. Overcome by fatigue and shame, he faints, later waking up in a cell where he is visited by a (somewhat improbable) procession of the novel's characters.

Bigger's first visitor is the Reverend Hammond, pastor of his mother's church. The reverend's speech about the importance of God and faith seems long-winded and meaningless. Bigger is unaffected by the pastor and inwardly rejects religious faith.

The next visitor is Jan Erlone. Bigger does not know what to make of Jan or his visit; he anticipates a desire for revenge on Jan's part and is surprised when Jan confesses that he himself was "kind of blind" the night they met. Bigger is further puzzled because Jan not only seems to understand him, but also to share a sense of guilt—if not for the crime itself, then for the formation of the criminal.

Jan offers his help and friendship to Bigger, introducing him to Boris Max of the Labor Defenders, who becomes Bigger's attorney. Max is drawn to the case by the Communist connection and sees in Bigger's predicament a situation of injustice prompted by political and economic brutality.

Mr. Dalton, who has come to the prison with Mrs. Dalton, confronts Max and tells him that he tried to help Bigger and will continue to help blacks despite Bigger's crimes. Max, however, chides him for the cosmetic nature of his charity.

Bigger's friends and family now arrive. His mother, both in her affection and her clinging to religious faith, inspires "shame" in Bigger. But it is through this visit of friends and family that Bigger realizes that he is not alone: "He had lived and acted on the assumption that he was alone, and now he saw that he had not been." Bigger's mother sees Mrs. Dalton and begs her to help Bigger. However, Mrs. Dalton replies that there is nothing they can do but promises not to make the Thomas family leave their apartment.

After everyone leaves, Buckley, the state's attorney, leads Bigger to a window, where he shows Bigger the crowds outside waiting to lynch him. He pressures Bigger to sign a confession and asks Bigger about Bessie, while trying to get him to confess to a series of other crimes he did not commit. Bigger eventually confesses, "[tracing] his every action," and, after he signs his confession, Buckley looks down at him scornfully, saying, "Just another scared colored boy from Mississippi."

Bigger is soon taken to the inquest, where the coroner produces Bessie's body as proof of Bigger's brutality. However, Bigger realizes that he is not really on trial for Bessie's death but that the "black girl [is] merely 'evidence'" for his murder of Mary.

After the inquest, Bigger is taken to the Dalton home for a reenactment of the crime. On his way to and from the house, mobs of angry whites yell and spit at him, and he sees a burning cross. Back at the jail, he is again visited by the reverend but throws his cross and yells, "Take your Jesus and go."

Max comes in to discuss Bigger's confession and his motivations for killing Mary and Bessie. Bigger tells him, "For a little while I was free . . . I killed 'em because I was scared and mad. But I had been scared and mad all my life and after I killed that first woman, I wasn't scared no more for a little while." Bigger voices his political and social alienation and underscores that there are many other young men like him. Max tells Bigger that at the arraignment they will enter a not-guilty plea, which they will then change to guilty at the trial in the hope of clemency.

After Max leaves, Bigger falls into a reverie, for the first time seeing whites as individual people. He has a vision of a "black sprawling prison" full of darkness, suffering, and isolation. Bigger realizes that there are many such cells and that perhaps he is the "equal of others." He has another vision of a "vast crowd of men" of all races, "with the sun melting away the differences." He craves a sense of "union, identity," a "wholeness, which had been denied to him all his life." He wants "to live now—not escape paying for his crime—but live in order to find out, to see if it were true. . . ."

In less then a week, Bigger is arraigned and tried. His plea of guilty is almost the only sound he utters during the trial, for Max serves as his representative and sole witness in the case, while Buckley in contrast calls sixty witnesses. The narrative skips over the testimony of most of Buckley's witnesses to Max's long and didactic speech in Bigger's defense. Max, building on Jan's sentiments, bases his case on the position that Bigger is essentially a product of his environment—that, separated and alienated from whites, he reacted in the only way he knew. In Max's speech, which reflects the ideas of the American Communist party, the state itself is placed on trial and held culpable for Bigger's actions: "The Negro boy's entire attitude toward life is a *crime!* The hate and fear we have inspired in him, woven by our civilization into the very structure of his consciousness . . . have become the justification of his existence." He also implicates Mr. Dalton and his capitalist real-estate practices in perpetuating the culture of hate and discrimination. Bigger is like the rat in the opening scenes of the novel: Fear and a sense of entrapment led him to react instinctively to his situation with violence.

Buckley's closing argument, on the other hand, calling for Bigger's conviction, focuses on his violence toward the state and society. The imagery that informs his language characterizes Bigger as less than human.

In the end, Bigger is sentenced to death; Max's attempts to obtain a pardon from the governor fail. In spite of his imminent execution, Bigger is moved by his experience with Max, who, like Jan, has told him to "believe in himself." However, the final conversation between the men is problematic. Bigger feels an affinity with and gratitude toward Max, and he refers to the questions Max had earlier asked him about his motivations. Max at first does not understand what Bigger is getting at, but Bigger tells him that even though Max knew Bigger was a murderer, he "treated [Bigger] like a man." Max asserts that Bigger's fundamental humanness was enough. Bigger tells Max that he did not mean to hurt anyone, that he was only "act[ing] hard," in response to others. He asks Max if the people who want to kill him feel the same way, but Max cannot answer the question and tells Bigger that he is going to die.

Max encourages Bigger to believe in himself, his own worth, and the validity of his feelings. His words express hope that one day those like Bigger will band together, "get angry and fight . . . to live again." Max tells Bigger that it is too late for him to work with others who are trying to "believe and make the world live again. . . . But it's not too late to believe what you felt, to understand what you felt. . . ." Bigger, he says, has always been told he was bad and so has believed it: "The job in getting people to fight and have faith is in making them believe what life has made them feel, making them feel that their feelings are as good as those of others." He tells Bigger that men "on both sides . . . are fighting for life" and that the side "with the most humanity" will win the struggle.

However, this is not what touches Bigger, who, in a sense, goes to his death believing that to live violently is to live freely. While he tells Max that he does believe in himself, his final words horrify the lawyer. He tells Max, "I didn't want to kill. . . . But what I killed for, I *am!*" He exclaims, "What I killed for must've been good! . . . I didn't know I was really alive in this world until I felt things hard enough to kill for 'em. . . ." He assures Max he feels "all right when [he] look[s] at it that way." Max, overcome with shock, "[gropes] for his hat like a blind man" and leaves. The novel closes with Bigger bidding the lawyer goodbye and smiling "a faint, wry bitter smile" as he hears "the ring of steel against steel as a far door [clangs] shut." ❖

—*Gary Pratt*
Bryn Mawr College

List of Characters

Bigger Thomas, the young African-American man who grows up in the slums of Chicago's South Side, is the protagonist of the novel, which traces his actions from his accidental and almost passionless murder of Mary Dalton to his arrest and execution. By linking his violence to social conditions, the text implies that Bigger is condemned before the crimes actually occur. Bigger's struggle is not merely to come to terms with his wrongdoing but to realize his position in society, the reasons for his violence, and his own dignity as a human being. He does this by seeing himself not as an isolated individual but as linked to the world, as both a product of an unjust political economy and a partner in a struggle with others.

The Thomas family, Bigger's mother, brother Buddy, and sister Vera, inhabit a run-down one-room apartment. While Bigger's relationship with his family is initially contentious, when they visit him in prison he realizes his connection to others.

Mr. Dalton, Mary's father and Bigger's employer, styles himself a generous and progressive philanthropist, but his real-estate business creates and sustains the very poverty his charitable acts aim to alleviate; in fact, he owns the rat-infested apartment rented by Bigger and his family. In this way, Mr. Dalton represents capitalism, in opposition to the voice of Communism in the character of Boris Max.

Mrs. Dalton, Mary's mother, is the most symbolic character: Through her blindness there is sight. She is often described in terms of whiteness; her presence in the text is radiant, ethereal, and ghostly. But it is for Bigger that her sight is most powerful and threatening: Her interruption of Bigger in Mary's room and his fear of her ability to sense his presence there fuel his rash act.

Mary Dalton is the wealthy young white woman whom Bigger murders. Although she is central to the novel's plot, her actual appearance in the novel is brief. She is the most transparent of characters: the archetypal rich young student who advocates racial and economic equality without truly understanding the issues.

Jan Erlone, although deeply affected by the murder of his girl-friend, Mary, is the character who first comes to understand Bigger. Initially, Jan, a member of the Communist party, appears to be shallow and hypocritical, but he surprises Bigger by not seeking revenge for Bigger's crime. Instead he introduces Bigger to Boris Max, the lawyer who agrees to defend Bigger.

Peggy, the Daltons' cook, presents the figure of the good servant, the poor white who makes better of herself. She initially tries to guide Bigger from his waywardness.

Bessie is Bigger's girlfriend, whom he also murders. Bessie's murder presents a paradox: It is a deliberate act but seems less heinous in the eyes of the law because Bessie is black and Mary is white. Nevertheless, Bessie's brutal murder means that Bigger's violence is pervasive; it is directed not just against whites, but against blacks, his own community, and intimates.

Britten is the private investigator the Daltons hire to investigate Mary's disappearance. When he discovers Communist pamphlets in Bigger's room, he becomes certain that the crime is part of a Communist conspiracy.

Boris Max, the lawyer who defends Bigger, helps him to realize his plight, his status as victim, and his human dignity. Max, who argues that brutality is linked to political and economic oppression, is also noticeably didactic and seems to articulate Wright's own ideas about racial difference and social justice, as well as the ideas of the American Communist party at the time Wright wrote his novel.

Buckley, the state's attorney, initially enters the text on a bill-board representation in book one. His vicious speech during the trial characterizes Bigger as depraved and inhuman.

Reverend Hammond, pastor of Bigger's mother's church, visits Bigger in prison but only repels him. ❖

Critical Views

MALCOLM COWLEY ON *NATIVE SON* AS A MESSAGE FOR
AMERICA

[Malcolm Cowley (1898–1989) was a distinguished
American poet and critic. He is the author of many
books, including *The Literary Situation* (1954), *A
Second Flowering* (1973), and *The Flower and the Leaf*
(1985). In this review of *Native Son,* Cowley recognizes
that Wright intended the novel as a message for
America: The country must come to terms with its
treatment of African Americans.]

Native Son is the most impressive American novel I have read
since *The Grapes of Wrath.* In some ways the two books
resemble each other: both deal with the dispossessed and both
grew out of the radical movement of the 1930's. There is, however, a distinction to be drawn between the motives of the two
authors. Steinbeck, more privileged than the characters in his
novel, wrote out of deep pity for them, and the fault he had to
avoid was sentimentality. Richard Wright, a Negro, was moved
by wrongs he had suffered in his own person, and what he had
to fear was a blind anger that might destroy the pity in him,
making him hate any character whose skin was whiter than his
own. His first book, *Uncle Tom's Children,* had not completely
avoided that fault. It was a collection of stories all but one of
which had the same pattern: a Negro was goaded into killing
one or more white men and was killed in turn, without feeling
regret for himself or his victims. Some of the stories I found
physically painful to read, even though I admired them. So
deep was the author's sense of the indignities heaped on his
race that one felt he was revenging himself by a whole series of
symbolic murders. In *Native Son* the pattern is the same, but
the author's sympathies have broadened and his resentment,
though not as deep, is less painful and personal.

The hero, Bigger Thomas, is a Negro boy of twenty: a pool-
room loafer, a bully, a liar and a petty thief. "Bigger, sometimes
I wonder why I birthed you," his pious mother tells him.
"Honest, you the most no-countest man I ever seen in all my

life." A Chicago philanthropist tries to help the family by hiring him as chauffeur. That same night Bigger kills the philanthropist's daughter—out of fear of being discovered in her room—and stuffs her body into the furnace. This half-accidental crlme leads to others. Bigger tries to cast the blame for the girl's disappearance on her lover, a Communist; he tries to collect a ransom from her parents; after the body is found he murders his Negro mistress to keep her from betraying him to the police. The next day he is captured on the snow-covered roof of a South Side tenement, while a mob howls in the street below.

In the last part of the book, which is also the best, we learn that the case of Bigger Thomas is not the author's deepest concern. Behind it is another, more complicated story he is trying hard to explain, though the words come painfully at first, and later come in a flood that almost sweeps him away. "Listen, you white folks," he seems to be saying over and over. "I want to tell you about all the Negroes in America. I want to tell you how they live and how they feel. I want you to change your minds about them before it is too late to prevent a worse disaster than any we have known. I speak for my own people, but I speak for America too." And because he does speak for and to the nation, without ceasing to be a Negro, his book has more force than any other American novel by a member of his race.

Bigger, he explains, had been trained from the beginning to be a bad citizen. He had been taught American ideals of life, in the schools, in the magazines, in the cheap movie houses, but had been denied any means of achieving them. Everything he wanted to have or do was reserved for the whites. "I just can't get used to it," he tells one of his poolroom buddies. "I swear to God I can't. . . . Every time I think about it I feel like somebody's poking a red-hot iron down my throat."

—Malcolm Cowley, "The Case of Bigger Thomas," *New Republic,* 18 March 1940, pp. 382–83

❖

JAMES BALDWIN ON BIGGER THOMAS AS A DESCENDANT OF UNCLE TOM

[James Baldwin (1924–1987) was one of the most respected African-American novelists of his generation. Among his many books are *Go Tell It on the Mountain* (1953) and *Giovanni's Room* (1956). In this extract from a celebrated essay on Stowe's *Uncle Tom's Cabin,* Baldwin argues that Bigger is a descendant of Uncle Tom in that he has unconsciously accepted the prevailing white view of black inferiority.]

It must be remembered that the oppressed and the oppressor are bound together within the same society; they accept the same criteria, they share the same beliefs, they both alike depend on the same reality. Within this cage it is romantic, more, meaningless, to speak of a "new" society as the desire of the oppressed, for that shivering dependence on the props of reality which he shares with the *Herrenvolk* makes a truly "new" society impossible to conceive. What is meant by a new society is one in which inequalities will disappear, in which vengeance will be exacted; either there will be no oppressed at all, or the oppressed and the oppressor will change places. But, finally, as it seems to me, what the rejected desire is, is an elevation of status, acceptance within the present community. Thus, the African, exile, pagan, hurried off the auction block and into the fields, fell on his knees before that God in Whom he must now believe; who had made him, but not in His image. This tableau, this impossibility, is the heritage of the Negro in America: *Wash me,* cried the slave to his Maker, *and I shall be whiter, whiter than snow!* For black is the color of evil; only the robes of the saved are white. It is this cry, implacable on the air and in the skull, that he must live with. Beneath the widely published catalogue of brutality—bringing to mind, somehow, an image, a memory of church-bells burdening the air—is this reality which, in the same nightmare notion, he both flees and rushes to embrace. In America, now, this country devoted to the death of the paradox—which may, therefore, be put to death by one—his lot is as ambiguous as a tableau by Kafka. To flee or not, to move or not, it is all the same; his doom is written on his forehead, it is carried in his heart. In *Native Son,* Bigger Thomas stands on a Chicago street corner watching airplanes flown by white men racing against the sun and "Goddamn" he says, the bitterness bubbling up like blood, remembering a million indignities, the terrible, rat-infested house, the humiliation of home-relief, the intense, aimless, ugly bickering, hating it; hatred smoulders through these pages like sulphur fire. All of Bigger's life is controlled, defined by his hatred and his fear. And later, his fear drives him to murder and his hatred to rape; he dies, having come, through this violence, we are told, for the first time, to a kind of life, having for the first time redeemed his manhood. Below the surface of this novel there lies, as it seems to me, a continuation, a complement of that monstrous legend it was written to destroy. Bigger is Uncle Tom's descendant, flesh of his flesh, so exactly opposite a portrait that, when the books are placed together, it seems that the contemporary Negro novelist and the dead New England woman ⟨Harriet Beecher Stowe⟩ are locked together in a deadly, timeless battle; the one uttering merciless exhortations, the other shouting curses. And, indeed, within this web of lust and fury, black and white can only thrust and counter-thrust, long for each other's slow, exquisite death; death by torture, acid, knives and burning; the thrust, the counter-thrust, the longing making the heavier that cloud which blinds and suffocates them both, so that they go down into the pit together. Thus has the cage betrayed us all, this moment, our life, turned to nothing through our terrible attempts to insure it. For Bigger's tragedy is not that he is cold or black or hungry, not even that he is American, black; but that he has accepted a theology that denies him life, that he admits the possibility of his being sub-human and feels constrained, therefore, to battle for his humanity according to those brutal criteria bequeathed him at his birth. But our humanity is our burden, our life; we need not battle for it; we need only to do what is infinitely more difficult—that is, accept it. The failure of the protest novel lies in its rejection of life, the human being, the denial of his beauty, dread, power, in its insistence that it is his categorization alone which is real and which cannot be transcended.

—James Baldwin, "Everybody's Protest Novel" (1949), *Notes of a Native Son* (Boston: Beacon Press, 1955), pp. 21–23

❖

ROBERT BONE ON NARRATIVE DRIVE AND SYMBOLISM IN
NATIVE SON

[Robert Bone (b. 1924), formerly the chairman of the
department of English at Columbia University Teachers
College, is the author of *Down Home: Origins of the
Afro-American Short Story* (1975) and the celebrated
treatise *The Negro Novel in America* (1958), from
which the following extract is taken. Here, Bone praises
the narrative drive of *Native Son* and also notes its
carefully worked out symbolism.]

The most impressive feature of *Native Son* is its narrative drive.
From the outset the novel assumes a fierce pace which carries
the reader breathlessly through Bigger's criminal career. Wright
allows as little interruption of the action as possible, with no
chapter divisions as such and only an occasional break to mark
a swift transition or change of scene. At the same time, he
writes with great economy, breaking with the comprehensive
and discursive tradition of the naturalistic novel. He provides
only three brief glimpses of Bigger's life prior to the main
action of the novel: his relationship with his family, with his
gang, and with his girl, Bessie. The reader must supply the rest,
for Wright's presentation is not direct but metaphorical.

On a literal level *Native Son* consists of three Books, dealing
with a murder, a flight and capture, and a trial. But the murder
and the circumstances which surround it are in reality an
extended metaphor, like the whale hunt in *Moby Dick*. The
novel is not to be read merely as the story of a gruesome
crime, though it is that. It is the hidden meaning of Bigger's
life, as revealed by the murder, which is the real subject of
Native Son. The novel is a modern epic, consisting of action on
the grand scale. As such, it functions as a commentary on the
more prosaic plane of daily living. ⟨. . .⟩

The successful fusion of narrative and metaphorical levels in
Native Son is only a sample of Wright's craftsmanship. Not the
least of his problems is to induce his readers to identify with
Bigger in spite of his monstrous crimes. This he accomplishes
by a tone which subtly controls and defines the reader's attitude toward Bigger. It is a tone of anguish and despair, estab-

lished at the outset by Wright's epigraph from the Book of Job: "Even today is my complaint rebellious; my stroke is heavier than my groaning." Thus the stark horror of *Native Son* is balanced by the spiritual anguish which, in a sense, produced it. This note of anguish, which emphasizes Bigger's suffering, is so intense as to be almost physical in character. It is sustained by a style which can only be called visceral. The author writes from his guts, describing the emotional state of his characters in graphic psychosomatic terms. It is a characteristic device which has its source in Wright's aching memory of the deep South.

Notwithstanding Wright's professed naturalism, the symbolic texture of *Native Son* is exceptionally rich. The whole novel is contained in the first few pages when Bigger, in unconscious anticipation of his own fate, corners a huge black rat and kills him with a skillet. Much of Wright's meaning is conveyed by appropriate "objective correlatives" for Bigger's inner feelings and emotions. The icy gales and heavy snowfalls of Books I and II represent a hostile white environment: "To Bigger and his kind white people were not really people; they were a sort of great natural force, like a stormy sky looming overhead." Throughout Book II the red glow of the furnace appears as a projection of Bigger's guilt. A series of breathing and choking images anticipates the manner of the murder, linking it symbolically to Bigger's choked and stifled life. There is a constant play on blindness, focused around the figure of Mrs. Dalton but aimed ultimately at the reader, who is expected to grope his way to an understanding of Bigger's life.

A lesser artist would have directed Bigger's symbolic revolt against a brutal oppressor, but Wright understands that such an approach would only make his audience feel smug and superior. He chooses as Bigger's victim a girl who is "friendly to Negroes," but whose kindness under the circumstances is a bitter mockery. By this device, Wright means to suggest that Bigger's sickness is too deep to be reached by kindness, and at the same time to involve his audience in responsibility for Bigger's crime. The Daltons, who are people of good will, hire Bigger because they "want to give Negroes a chance." But they also own real estate on the South side, and have thus helped to make the black ghetto what it is. They are, in short, just as innocent and just as guilty as we.

Book I portrays the old Bigger; Book II, the new; Book III, the Bigger who might have been. The bare narrative is concerned with Bigger's fight for his life, but the dramatic tension of Book III is centered elsewhere. The important question is not whether Bigger will be spared, but whether he will be saved. Bigger's impending death in the electric chair is simply the crisis which forces a resolution of his inner conflict, thus revealing what is basic in his personality. After his talk with the lawyer, Max—the most intimate of his life—Bigger feels that he must make a decision: "In order to walk to that chair he had to weave his feelings into a hard shield of either hope or hate. To fall between them would mean living and dying in a fog of fear." On what terms will Bigger die; in hope or in hate? This is the tension of Book III.

> —Robert Bone, *The Negro Novel in America* (New Haven: Yale University Press, 1958), pp. 144–48

❖

IRVING HOWE ON *NATIVE SON* AS AN ATTACK ON BOTH WHITES AND BLACKS

[Irving Howe (1920–1993) was one of the leading literary and cultural critics of the century. He wrote many books, including *Politics and the Novel* (1957), *The Critical Point: On Literature and Culture* (1973), and *World of Our Fathers* (1976). In this extract, Howe, commenting in part on James Baldwin's essay, maintains that *Native Son* is a gauntlet thrown down both at whites (for their oppression of blacks) and blacks (for the price they have paid for their oppression).]

The day *Native Son* appeared, American culture was changed forever. No matter how much qualifying the book might later need, it made impossible a repetition of the old lies. In all its crudeness, melodrama and claustrophobia of vision, Richard Wright's novel brought out into the open, as no one ever had before, the hatred, fear and violence that have crippled and may yet destroy our culture.

A blow at the white man, the novel forced him to recognize himself as an oppressor. A blow at the black man, the novel forced him to recognize the cost of his submission. *Native Son* assaulted the most cherished of American vanities: the hope that the accumulated injustice of the past would bring with it no lasting penalties, the fantasy that in his humiliation the Negro somehow retained a sexual potency—or was it a child-like good-nature?—that made it necessary to envy and still more to suppress him. Speaking from the black wrath of retribution, Wright insisted that history can be a punishment. He told us the one thing even the most liberal whites preferred not to hear: that Negroes were far from patient or forgiving, that they were scarred by fear, that they hated every moment of their suppression even when seeming most acquiescent, and that often enough they hated *us*, the decent and cultivated white men who from complicity or neglect shared in the responsibility for their plight. If such younger novelists as Baldwin and Ralph Ellison were to move beyond Wright's harsh naturalism and toward more supple modes of fiction, that was possible only because Wright had been there first, courageous enough to release the full weight of his anger.

In *Black Boy,* the autobiographical narrative he published several years later, Wright would tell of an experience he had while working as a bellboy in the South. Many times he had come into a hotel room carrying luggage or food and seen naked white women lounging about, unmoved by shame at his presence, for "blacks were not considered human beings any-way . . . I was a non-man . . . I felt doubly cast out." With the publication of *Native Son,* however, Wright forced his readers to acknowledge his anger, and in that way, if none other, he wrested for himself a sense of dignity as a man. He forced his readers to confront the disease of our culture, and to one of its most terrifying symptoms he gave the name of Bigger Thomas.

Brutal and brutalized, lost forever to his unexpended hatred and his fear of the world, a numbed and illiterate black boy stumbling into a murder and never, not even at the edge of the electric chair, breaking through to an understanding of either his plight or himself, Bigger Thomas was a part of Richard Wright, a part even of the James Baldwin who stared with hor-ror at Wright's Bigger, unable either to absorb him into his consciousness or eject him from it. Enormous courage, a discipline of self-conquest, was required to conceive Bigger Thomas, for this was no eloquent Negro spokesman, no admirable intellectual or formidable proletarian. Bigger was drawn—one would surmise, deliberately—from white fantasy and white contempt. Bigger was the worst of Negro life accepted, then rendered a trifle conscious and thrown back at those who had made him what he was. "No American Negro exists," Baldwin would later write, "who does not have his private Bigger Thomas living in the skull."

Wright drove his narrative to the very core of American phobia: sexual fright, sexual violation. He understood that the fantasy of rape is a consequence of guilt, what the whites suppose themselves to deserve. He understood that the white man's notion of uncontaminated Negro vitality, little as it had to do with the bitter realities of Negro life, reflected some ill-formed and buried feeling that our culture has run down, lost its blood, become febrile. And he grasped the way in which the sexual issue has been intertwined with social relationships, for even as the white people who hire Bigger as their chauffeur are decent and charitable, even as the girl he accidentally kills is a liberal of sorts, theirs is the power and the privilege. "We black and they white. They got things and we ain't. They do things and we can't."

The novel barely stops to provision a recognizable social world, often contenting itself with cartoon simplicities and yielding almost entirely to the nightmare incomprehension of Bigger Thomas. The mood is apocalyptic, the tone superbly aggressive. Wright was an existentialist long before he heard the name, for he was committed to the literature of extreme situations both through the pressures of his rage and the gasping hope of an ultimate catharsis.

Wright confronts both the violence and the crippling limitations of Bigger Thomas. For Bigger white people are not people at all, but something more, "a sort of great natural force, like a stormy sky looming overhead." And only through violence does he gather a little meaning in life, pitifully little: "he had murdered and created a new life for himself." Beyond that Bigger cannot go.

—Irving Howe, "Black Boys and Native Sons," *A World More Attractive: A View of Modern Literature and Politics* (New York: Horizon Press, 1963), pp. 100–103

❖

RALPH ELLISON ON WRIGHT, BALDWIN, AND HOWE

[Ralph Ellison (1914–1994), an important black American novelist and author of *Invisible Man* (1952), also wrote a small body of literary criticism. In this extract, Ellison counters the assertion of Irving Howe that Richard Wright made much subsequent African-American literature possible, but he recognizes the greatness of *Native Son* and confesses to an admiration of Wright himself.]

Wright believed in the much abused idea that novels are "weapons"—the counterpart of the dreary notion, common among most minority groups, that novels are instruments of good public relations. But I believe that true novels, even when most pessimistic and bitter, arise out of an impulse to celebrate human life and therefore are ritualistic and ceremonial at their core. Thus they would preserve as they destroy, affirm as they reject.

In *Native Son,* Wright began with the ideological proposition that what whites think of the Negro's reality is more important than what Negroes themselves know it to be. Hence Bigger Thomas was presented as a near-subhuman indictment of white oppression. He was designed to shock whites out of their apathy and end the circumstances out of which Wright insisted Bigger emerged. Here environment is all—and interestingly enough, environment conceived solely in terms of the physical, the non-conscious. Well, cut off my legs and call me

Shorty! Kill my parents and throw me on the mercy of the court as an orphan! Wright could imagine Bigger, but Bigger could not possibly imagine Richard Wright. Wright saw to that.

But without arguing Wright's right to his personal vision, I would say that he was himself a better argument for my approach than Bigger was for his. And so, to be fair and as inclusive as Howe, is James Baldwin. Both are true Negro Americans, and both affirm the broad possibility of personal realization which I see as a saving aspect of American life. Surely, this much can be admitted without denying the injustice which all three of us have protested.

Howe is impressed by Wright's pioneering role and by the ". . . enormous courage, the discipline of self-conquest required to conceive Bigger Thomas. . . ." And earlier: "If such younger novelists as Baldwin and Ralph Ellison were able to move beyond Wright's harsh naturalism toward more supple modes of fiction, that was only possible because Wright has been there first, courageous enough to release the full weight of his anger."

It is not for me to judge Wright's courage, but I must ask just why it was possible for me to write as I write "only" because Wright released his anger? Can't I be allowed to release my own? What does Howe know of my acquaintance with violence, or the shape of my courage or the intensity of my anger? I suggest that my credentials are at least as valid as Wright's, even though he began writing long before I did, and it is possible that I have lived through and committed even more violence than he. Howe must wait for an autobiography before he can be responsibly certain. Everybody wants to tell us what a Negro is, yet few wish, even in a joke, to be one. But if you would tell me who I am, at least take the trouble to discover what I have been. ⟨. . .⟩

No, Wright was no spiritual father of mine, certainly in no sense I recognize—nor did he pretend to be, since he felt that I had started writing too late. It was Baldwin's career, not mine, that Wright proudly advanced by helping him attain the Eugene Saxton Fellowship, and it was Baldwin who found Wright a lion in his path. Being older and familiar with quite different lions in quite different paths, I simply stepped around him.

But Wright was a friend for whose magazine I wrote my first book review and short story, and a personal hero in the same way Hot Lips Paige and Jimmy Rushing were friends and heroes. I felt no need to attack what I considered the limitations of his vision because I was quite impressed by what he had achieved. And in this, although I saw with the black vision of Ham, I was, I suppose, as pious as Shem and Japheth. Still I would write my own books and they would be in themselves, implicitly, criticisms of Wright's; just as all novels of a given historical moment form an argument over the nature of reality and are, to an extent, criticisms each of the other.

While I rejected Bigger Thomas as any *final* image of Negro personality, I recognized *Native Son* as an achievement; as one man's essay in defining the human condition as seen from a specific Negro perspective at a given time in a given place. And I was proud to have known Wright and happy for the impact he had made upon our apathy. But Howe's ideas notwithstanding, history is history, cultural contacts ever mysterious, and taste exasperatingly personal.

—Ralph Ellison, "The World and the Jug" (1963), *Shadow and Act* (New York: Random House, 1964), pp. 114–15, 117–18

❖

DAN MCCALL ON THE CRITICAL RECEPTION OF *NATIVE SON*

[Dan McCall (b. 1940), a professor of American studies at Cornell University, is also a novelist and literary critic. Among his critical works are *The Silence of Bartleby* (1989) and *The Example of Richard Wright* (1969), from which the following extract is taken. Here, McCall discusses the critical reception of *Native Son* and examines Wright's own statements about the intentions of the work.]

Bigger Thomas was no Raskolnikov, no Dostoevskyan hero who at least had some massive (albeit depraved) intellectual force behind his act of killing. Bigger had no *Übermensch* leading him on; no Idea had twisted his humanity. He killed because everything in his life had wrung humanity out of him and he only wanted to become a one-man lynch mob. He was playing Massa. Running and helpless and trapped, he suddenly crowned himself the Destroyer King. In the beginning he said on the slum streets that he would like to fly; murder presented itself as his airplane. The reviewers paid tribute to the enormous power of the narrative, but several of them questioned Wright's intellectual and moral apprehension of what that power meant. In the *Saturday Review of Literature* (March 2, 1940), Jonathan Daniels said that here was a good hard-boiled story of a rat, but it was only "the very ancient story of all criminals," not an indictment of America, for "every order creates its rats and rebels." Another critic, Charles Glicksberg, said that it was "sheer nonsense to insist that the act of killing made Bigger free, made him feel that his actions were important." Besides, Glicksberg went on, "Wright is holding a loaded pistol at the head of the white world while he mutters between clenched teeth: 'Either you grant us equal rights as human beings or else this is what will happen.'" And that is a "dangerous doctrine to pour into the susceptible minds of frustrated young Negro readers, who are resentful enough as it is." And David L. Cohn in the *Atlantic* said that Wright was exaggerating—look at how many Negroes have made a success in the United States—and Wright had succumbed to "blinding" hate worthy of the Ku Klux Klan. Ben Burns would later speak in the *Reporter* of Wright's "Hate School of Literature." Zora Hurston had complained of "Long Black Song" in *Uncle Tom's Children* that it held "lavish killing here, perhaps enough to satisfy all male black readers" and now this new novel seemed to hold enough for even the whites. Everywhere critics were objecting to the message, and everywhere people were buying the book.

In "How Bigger Was Born" Wright tries to solve some of the mysteries as to where his great "bad nigger" came from. He lists various black boys in the South whom he had known as a child, calling them Biggers 1, 2, 3, 4, and 5. Three of them were both crude and cruel, helplessly lost in compulsive violence; two were proud, giving the whites a dose of their own medicine. Over the years these various boys came together, Wright said, and lay as one form, "an undeveloped negative" that he carried with him up North, "a negative that lay in the back of my mind." Wright seems to say, in his essay, that it is impossible to separate legitimate rebellion from sadism because dignity was obtainable for his black boys only by acts of prideful destruction. His Bigger 5 pulled a knife on the conductor in a Jim Crow streetcar. When the conductor backed down, the other Negroes in the car "experienced an intense flash of pride." He goes farther than that, saying that the "good niggers," the black people in the South who had education and money—and therefore, perhaps, a piece of the white monopoly on humanity—were only what their names implied, "good niggers," passively ignoring the plight of their black brothers. Wright says, "The Bigger Thomases were the *only* Negroes I know of who consistently violated the Jim Crow laws of the South. . . ." (My emphasis.)

Now it is surely true that, as E. R. Embree has said, "Richard Wright wanted to write not a book but a bomb." And it is also true that Wright, like his fictional creation, had an obsession with violence. Toward the end of *Black Boy* Wright says that "it was perhaps an accident that I had never killed." And in "How Bigger Was Born" he confesses of the Bigger 1, "Maybe I longed secretly to be like him." Nelson Algren said in his review that "Thomas forced recognition by an act of murder, Wright by an act of art," the implication being that it was very lucky Wright was able to educate himself, to have a "socially approved" outlet for his violence so that he could murder on paper instead of in the flesh. And when Samuel Sillen ran a series on " 'Native Son': Pros and Cons" in the *New Masses,* other black men of letters came to the defense of Wright's portrait of racial hate; Chester Himes said that Bigger "had to hate them to keep himself a human being, knowing that when he gave in to being afraid of them without hating them he would lose everything which impelled his desire to fly a plane or build a bridge." Yet Wright himself was disturbed that in the controversy too many readers and critics had been extremely careless in their understanding of what Bigger's hate meant and how he, the author, had portrayed it. Wright was moved to passionate italics in the *Atlantic* (June 1940): "No *advocacy* of hate is in that book. *None!*"

Bigger is "the beast in the skull." The difficulty in thinking clearly and talking clearly about "the beast in the skull" is that one can become so intensely, obsessively conscious of it that one lets it out, lets it out not to expose it but to let it do its damage. If one lives too long and too carelessly with the beast, one can love it. After fighting it for so long, after hating it so deeply, one feels something break inside; the hate turns to love, the fierce denial turns to passionate embrace. It is an enormously complicated problem for the black writer, trying to make sense of himself and his world. Wrestling in such agony with the beast he may begin to pump it. Becoming an intellectual Bigger Thomas, he deals in fantasies without ever seeing them for what they are. How Wright faced the problem in *Native Son* involves the question of what kind of book it is, and when one looks carefully at it one can see several indications that Wright is trying to understand the fantasy for what it is and provide some imaginative controls to direct its power.

—Dan McCall, *The Example of Richard Wright* (New York: Harcourt, Brace & World, 1969), pp. 64–67

❖

EDWARD MARGOLIES ON WRIGHT'S VISION OF RACE AND SOCIAL CHANGE

[Edward Margolies (b. 1925) is a former professor of English and American studies at the College of Staten Island of the City University of New York. He has written *Native Sons* (1968), a study of twentieth-century African-American literature, and *Which Way Did He Go? The Private Eye in Dashiell Hammett, Raymond Chandler, Chester Himes, and Ross Macdonald* (1982). In this extract from *The Art of Richard Wright* (1969), Margolies explores Wright's vision of race in *Native Son*.]

Bigger's crimes then signify something beyond their therapeutic value. In a world without God, without rules, without order, purpose, or meaning, each man becomes his own god and creates his own world in order to exist. Bigger acts violently in order to exist and it is perhaps this fact, rather than his continued undying hatred of whites, that so terrifies Max at the close of the novel. It is possible that Max senses that as a Communist he too has worked hard to dispense with the old social order— but the metaphysical vacuum that has been created does not necessarily lead men like Bigger to Communism, but may just as easily lead to the most murderous kind of nihilism. Max's horror was to become Wright's dilemma two years after the publication of *Native Son* when Wright himself would leave the Party. Wright could no longer accept the assumptions of Communism any more than he could those of racist America. Yet the prospects of a new world of positive meaning and value seemed very distant indeed.

It is then in the roles of a Negro nationalist revolutionary and a metaphysical rebel that Wright most successfully portrays Bigger. And it is from these aspects of Bigger's character rather than from any Marxist interpretation that Wright's sociology really emerges. For the metaphor that Wright uses best to illustrate the relationship between the races is "blindness"—and blindness is one result of Bigger's racist nationalist pride. Prior to his conversion by murder Bigger has blinded himself to the realities of Negro life as well as to the humanity of whites. As in *Uncle Tom's Children,* he vaguely discerns the white enemy as "white tides," "white blurs," "icy white walls," and "looming white mountains." He is therefore unable to accept Jan's offer of friendship, because he blindly regards all whites as symbols of oppression. It is only after his metaphysical rebellion has been effected by the death of the two girls that Bigger acquires sight. When he looks at his family, he sees them now as blind as he had been; he understands what it means to be a Negro. Buddy, his brother "was blind . . . Buddy, too, went round and round in a groove and did not see things. Buddy's clothes hung loosely compared with the way Jan's hung. Buddy seemed aimless, lost, with no sharp or hard edges, like a chubby puppy . . . he saw in Buddy a certain stillness, an isolation, meaninglessness." When he looks at his mother he sees "how soft and shapeless she was. . . . She moved about slowly, touching objects with her fingers as she passed them, using them for support. . . . There was in her heart, it seemed, a heavy and delicately balanced burden whose weight she did not want to assume by disturbing it one whit." His sister, Vera "seemed to be shrinking from life in every gesture she made. The very manner in which she sat showed a fear so deep as to be an organic part of her."

Bigger's new vision enables him to see how whites see him as well—or more precisely, how blind whites are to his humanity, his existence. Whites prefer to think of Negroes in easily stereotyped images—in images of brute beast or happy minstrel. They are incapable of viewing black men as possessing sensitivity and intelligence. And it is this blindness that Bigger counts on as the means of getting away with his crimes. When he schemes with Bessie to collect ransom money from the Daltons, he tells her the (white) police would never suspect them because they "think niggers is too scared." And even well-meaning people like Mr. and Mrs. Dalton are blind to the sufferings of Negroes. Believing that acts of charity can somehow miraculously banish in Negroes feelings of shame, fear, and suspicion, the Daltons lavish millions of dollars on Negro colleges and welfare organizations—while at the same time they continue to support a rigid caste system that is responsible for the Negroes' degradation in the first place. Mrs. Dalton's blindness is symbolic of the blindness of the white liberal philanthropic community. Additionally, the Communists, Mary, Jan, and Max, are just as blind to the humanity of Negroes as the others—even though they presumably want to enlist Negroes as equals in their own cause. For Mary and Jan, Bigger is an abstraction—a symbol of exploitation rather than someone whose feelings they have ever really tried to understand. Although he does not know it, this is really the reason Bigger hates them. Even when Mary concedes her blindness, she has no idea how condescending she sounds to Bigger. "Never in my life have I been inside of a Negro home, yet they must live like we live. They're human."

In the final analysis *Native Son* stands on shifting artistic grounds. Had Wright managed to affix a different ending more in accord with the character of Bigger and the philosophical viewpoint he seeks to embody, the novel might have emerged a minor masterpiece. Yet, for all its faults, *Native Son* retains surprising power. The reasons are still not clearly understood by even present-day critics. It is not simply that what has been called the Negro problem has once more intruded itself into the national consciousness, if not the national conscience—although "sociology" should certainly not be discounted as an important factor. Nor is it merely the sensational nature of the crimes Bigger committed, compounded as they were with racial and sexual overtones. In part, of course, it is the terrible excitement, the excruciating suspense of flight and pursuit that Wright invests in his best prose. In part, too, it is the shock of unembellished hatred in Wright's portrayal of a seemingly nondescript apathetic Negro boy.

> —Edward Margolies, *The Art of Richard Wright* (Carbondale: Southern Illinois University Press, 1969), pp. 116–19

❖

ROGER ROSENBLATT ON REALITY AND BLINDNESS IN *NATIVE SON*

[Roger Rosenblatt (b. 1940) is an author, journalist, and editor who has written for the *New Republic, Washington Post, Time, U.S. News and World Report,* and "The MacNeil/Lehrer Newshour." He is the author of *The Children of War* (1983) and *Witness: The World Since Hiroshima* (1985). In this extract from *Black Fiction* (1974), Rosenblatt explores the metaphorical uses of reality and blindness in *Native Son.*]

The question is, where is Bigger's real life, and how is it to be distinguished from the varieties of unreality in which he lives? Bigger enjoys the world of the movies, not only the movies themselves, but the movie houses as well, which provide the atmosphere of kings in royal boxes (the theater he goes to is called The Regal) and the darkness that makes Bigger inconspicuous. Yet even the movie (dream) house is not safe from Buckley. At the trial Buckley reveals not only that Bigger went to the movies on the day of the murder, but that he sneaked in without paying. Nor is it only Buckley who invades the movie world, but reality as well. One of the films Bigger watches is about Communists and millionaires. The second is *Trader Horn,* about Africa, but Bigger only wants to think about the story of the "smart people," *The Gay Woman*. Gus tells him that "rich, white women'll go to bed with anybody, from a poodle on up. Shucks, they even have their chauffeurs." Bigger daydreams:

> Yes, his going to work for the Daltons was something big. Maybe Mr. Dalton was a millionaire. Maybe he had a daughter who was a hot kind of girl; maybe she spent lots of money; maybe she'd like to come to the south side and see the sights sometimes. Or maybe she had a secret sweetheart and only he would know about it because he would have to drive her around; maybe she would give him money not to tell.

The terrible aspect of this conjecture, of course, is that it all, or most of it, comes true. The satisfaction of the daydream perverts the dream into a nightmare. When the movies are over, Gus remarks, "Swell, wasn't it?" Bigger answers, "Yeah. It was a killer."

In the madhouse people do not wish to be looked at, and yet in one way or another everyone is blind, so the fear of exposure is groundless. In all cases but Mrs. Dalton's, blindness is psychosomatic, but like the others, Mrs. Dalton has a spiritual handicap as well as a physical one. A latter-day Grandissime, she and her husband, as Max points out, cannot see the malevolent condition which they serve and perpetuate. Similarly, Mary and Jan cannot see the emptiness of their charity. Bessie is blinded by tears and fright. At different times Bigger is blinded by snow, light, and rage. In the presence of Jan and Max he feels "transparent," invisible. At the end of the novel Max "groped for his hat like a blind man." The two abstract conceptions which inform *Native Son*, love and justice, are also traditionally blind.

Only one person, Bigger, gains a kind of sight in the novel, but the vision which Bigger gains is also distorted. It is made up of the images that appear when one holds a magnifying glass close to the face, and then moves it further and further away from one's eyes until the picture reflected in the glass comes in at once clearly and upside down. Bigger begins the story seeing everything in a haze. The sight which he eventually achieves is in sharp focus, but out of whack:

> He felt in the quiet presence of his brother, mother, and sister a force, inarticulate and unconscious, making for living without

thinking, making for peace and habit, making for a hope that blinded. He felt that they wanted and yearned to see life in a certain way; they needed a certain picture of the world; there was one way of living they preferred above all others; and they were blind to what did not fit. They did not want to see what others were doing if that doing did not feed their own desires. All one had to do was be bold, do something nobody thought of. The whole thing came to him in the form of a powerful and simple feeling; there was in everyone a great hunger to believe that made him blind, and if he could see while others were blind, then he could get what he wanted and never be caught at it. Now, who on earth would think that he, a black timid Negro boy, would murder and burn a rich white girl and would sit and wait for his breakfast like this? Elation filled him.

It is perfectly apt for Bigger to watch Jan and Mary, as he does, through a rearview mirror, because the final understanding which he reaches of Jan and of Mary, of the Daltons, Max, of the entire white world and his relation to it, is completely turned around: "What I killed for must've been good."

Everything is turned around in this way in *Native Son,* even the idea of color. Here darkness, customarily connected with evil, dishonor, or ignorance, offers safety, whereas whiteness is a source of terror. In black fiction generally, white is the color of suffocation, disorientation, deafness, blindness, of threat, of being cornered. It is also the non-color by which all others, including black, may be swallowed up. In *Beetlecreek,* William Demby cites "the shriveled paleness" of Trapp's soul. In *dem,* William Kelley's Harlem girls chant about a polar bear coming to enslave them. The domineering chef in Claude McKay's *Home to Harlem* prizes the whiteness of his uniform, as does Mr. Watford, the man without feeling, in Paule Marshall's "Barbados" (*Soul Clap Hands and Sing*). Glory, the shrew of Ann Petry's *Country Place,* is described solely by the blondness of her hair. John Grimes (*Go Tell It on the Mountain*) "knew that time was indifferent, like snow and ice." In Wright, white signifies nothingness: "to Bigger and his kind white people were not really people; they were a sort of great natural force, like a stormy sky looming overhead."

—Roger Rosenblatt, *Black Fiction* (Cambridge, MA: Harvard University Press, 1974), pp. 26–29

❖

[Dorothy S. Redden is a former professor of English at Douglass College, Rutgers University. In this extract, Redden defends Wright against the claims of some critics who accuse *Native Son* of being excessively melodramatic and of sowing divisive racial hatred. She argues instead that the work is both controlled and emotionally powerful.]

⟨. . .⟩ the charge that *Native Son* is emotionally abandoned cannot be supported. Books I and II are certainly dramatic, if not melodramatic. From the hysterical killing of the huge fanged black rat in the crowded apartment to the shootout on top of the ice-covered water tank, the narrative whirls forward on a flood of surging feelings. Authentic passion there is, but the issue is not so much what Wright felt as how he disciplined, or failed to discipline, what he felt. How could a man who was "choked" with any emotions, let alone rage and hatred, produce a novel of this caliber? Wright may well have harbored powerful feelings, but he was not having some sort of lengthy tantrum when he constructed the coherent, meaningful, expressive story of Bigger Thomas.

Think what Wright might have done with uncontrolled emotions in this novel, and did not. He did not make his whites hateable. The worst one can say of the various Daltons is that they are literally or figuratively blind; they are not "evil." Even Buckley, the prosecutor, is more stupid than satanic. And it is a white man, Max, who is clearly intended to be the most intelligent and humane person in the book—the author's spokesman for the truth.

Wright did not fill up his stage with angelic, appealing Blacks, either—least of all his protagonist. He might have drawn a gentle, suffering martyr-Bigger or a grand Othello-Bigger of noble character and intellect, or even a modest, everyday sort of Bigger. Instead he created almost a stereotype of the skulking Black brute who violates and kills pale virgins in their beds. Wright does not stop with the stifling of Mary, which might be interpreted as a horrible accident; he makes

Bigger murder Bessie, his girl, in an even more gruesome way. Nor does Wright flinch from the sexual overtones in either case; here too he meets the myths head on. Surely a Black writer in the grip of violent passions would have invented a different sort of Black protagonist.

And why, if Wright were simply vengeful, did he not fully exploit Bigger's treatment at the hands of callous whites? There is some of that, to be sure, particularly in the fear-crazed mob in Book III. But on the whole Wright exercises restraint. He might have included some graphic police brutality, for instance, between the time of Bigger's capture and the beginning of his trial—beatings, tortures, perversions. Wright chooses to mention only one small detail: that somewhere, somehow, in the chaos, Bigger lost two fingernails, he does not know how.

Again, why did Wright consciously reject, as he has stated explicitly, his original ending for the book, which showed Bigger strapped and waiting in the electric chair? Wright was not carried away by his emotions, and he did not want his readers to be so, either; we are not intended to dissolve in pity or fear, but to see clearly. The stress was not to be on the pathos or cruelty of Bigger's death, but on its meaning, on what Wright called "the moral . . . horror of Negro life in the United States."

Native Son is not choked with rage, hatred, or vengefulness. It is taut with emotion, but that emotion is contained and transcended. Certainly Richard Wright was a man of scalding feelings which inevitably found their way into his work. But he knew what he was about in *Native Son,* and one accepts his flat, exasperated, explicit refutation of Mr. Cohn's reading: "No *advocacy* of hate is in that book. *None!*" The italics are his own.

—Dorothy S. Redden, "Richard Wright and *Native Son:* Not Guilty," *Black American Literature Forum* 10, No. 4 (Winter 1976): 111–12

❖

SHERLEY ANNE WILLIAMS ON *NATIVE SON* AND AFRICAN-AMERICAN LITERATURE

[Sherley Anne Williams (b. 1944) is a professor of Afro-American literature at the University of California at San Diego. She is also a poet, novelist, and literary critic and the author of *Give Birth to Brightness: A Thematic Study of Neo-Black Literature* (1972). In this extract, Williams argues that *Native Son* is the model for contemporary African-American novelists but criticizes the depiction of black women in the novel.]

Richard Wright is the father of modern Afro-American literature. His most famous novel, *Native Son* (1940), is seen in some quarters as "the model" for contemporary black novelists, his autobiographical narrative, *Black Boy* (1945), as the text that authenticates "the extraordinary articulate self that lies behind" this most famous novel of black privation and rage. *Native Son* began an era of new realism in Afro-American fiction, as black writers, inspired by the thrilling example of Wright, exposed the filth, corruption, and depravity of urban slums that, together with American racism, stunted and deformed the blacks forced to live in them. In his nonfiction work, *Twelve Million Black Voices* (1941), *Black Power* (1954), and *White Man Listen!* (1957), Wright documented the social and psychological effects on and reactions of black and other Third World peoples forced to live under the oppression of internal and external colonialism. In doing so, he took upon himself the task of being spokesman for some twelve million black people in America. And if his art suffered, as some critics have charged, because of this political spokesmanship, he at least made it possible to admit, explore, and thus move beyond the almost elemental expression of rage that drives *Native Son* to its powerful climax. But Wright also fathered a bastard line, racist misogyny—the denigration of black women as justification for glorifying the symbolic white woman—and male narcissism—the assumption that racism is a crime against the black man's sexual expression rather than an economic, political, and psychological crime against black people—that was to flower in the fiction of black writers in the late sixties and early seventies.

Women are only supporting players with bit parts in Wright's fiction. The women in *Native Son,* for example, are all cardboard figures: the white woman, Mary Dalton, whom Bigger Thomas accidentally kills, was never meant to transcend the symbolism of American fruit forbidden the black man; and Bigger's girlfriend, Bessie, whom he murders with malice aforethought, represents nothingness, a meaningless void that Bigger's killings allow him to rise above. Bigger's mother and his sister represent modern versions of toming and accommodation. We excuse these characterizations within the context of the novel because of the power of Wright's psychological portrait of Bigger; this is Bigger's story, and not even the introduction of an articulate white male character, Bigger's lawyer Max who, in a twenty-page speech, attempts to summarize something of what Wright had rendered (often brilliantly and beautifully) in the preceding two hundred and fifty pages, can diminish Bigger's presence in the novel. Because the characterization of women in Wright's novels is so limited, one must turn to Wright's stories in order to understand both the range and the issues involved in these portrayals. Wright never, in his published work, moves beyond these early characterizations of black women.

— Sherley Anne Williams, "Papa Dick and Sister Woman: Reflections on Women in the Fiction of Richard Wright," *American Novelists Revisited: Essays in Feminist Criticism,* ed. Fritz Fleishmann (Boston: G. K. Hall, 1982), pp. 396–97

❖

A. ROBERT LEE ON NARRATIVE DEVICES IN *NATIVE SON*

[A. Robert Lee (b. 1941) is a senior lecturer in English literature at the University of Canterbury in England. He is the editor of *Black Fiction: New Studies in the Afro-American Novel Since 1945* (1980) and *The Modern American Novella* (1989). In this extract, Lee examines the urban landscape of *Native Son* and some other significant narrative devices used by Wright.]

It has been objected to *Native Son,* in part by James Baldwin, that it reads as though set in something of a historical vacuum, its principal characters unsatisfactorily one-dimensional and without sufficient human resonance. To the extent that this is true, it suggests not so much weakness as the fact that Wright was attempting narrative markedly different from that assumed to be naturalistic; he was in fact as much writing his own version of the kind of narration he mentions as the line of Poe, Hawthorne and Dostoyevsky. The landscape of the novel, for instance, certainly proposes a real Chicago but also and in matching degree a Chicago of the mind and senses, the bleak outward urban landscape of *Native Son* as the correlative of Bigger's psyche. His violence, from the opening episode with the rat and his bullying of his poolhall friends through to the murder and incineration of Mary and his flight, takes its course as the expression of his turbulence within. It serves as his one form of self-articulation. *Native Son* thus should be read as exploring psychology and human personality in a manner as close to, say, Kafka, as to Dreiser or Steinbeck, the Chicago of the novel as much the expression of the displaced city pent up inside Bigger as the Windy City of actuality. In arguing for this more 'shadowed' reading of *Native Son,* three supporting kinds of allusion must do duty for the novel's procedures as a whole: they have to do with sight, with the image of Bigger as rat, and with exactly the kind of city depicted in *Native Son.*

Not only 'The Man Who Lived Underground' but *Native Son,* too, calls up *Invisible Man* in its handling of seeing and sightlessness, typically in a passage like the following in which Bigger considers the implication of having killed Mary:

> No, he did not have to hide behind a wall or a curtain now; he had a safer way of being safe, an easier way. What he had done last night had proved that. Jan was blind. Mary had been blind. Mr. Dalton had been blind. And Mrs. Dalton was blind; yes, blind in more ways than one. . . . Bigger felt that a lot of people were like Mrs. Dalton, blind. . . .

Just as Bigger's black world sees him one way—merely wayward if his hard-pressed mother is to be believed, a tough street-companion according to his poolhall buddies, a lover in Bessie's eyes—so, too, to the white world he is seen only through part of his identity, as some preferred invention like the recipient of Mr. Dalton's self-serving largesse, or the proletarian black worker imagined by Mary and her lover Jan, or Mr. Max's example of how 'scientific' history shapes the individual consciousness. Even the final chase scenes across rundown wasteland Chicago against which he is silhouetted by the police cross-lights show him only in part, the formulaic rapist-murderer. Bigger's full human self, even at the end probably ungrasped by the victim himself, lies locked inside 'the faint, wry bitter smile' he wears to his execution. Perhaps the true self lies teasingly present in the white cat which watches him burn Mary's body (an episode to recall the duplicitous intentions of stories like 'Ethan Brand' or 'The Masque of the Red Death'), in part the emissary of the white world which has hitherto so defined Bigger but just as plausibly the rarest glimpse of his own fugitive and 'whited' identity.

The rat killed by Bigger in the opening chapter also sets up a motif which resonates throughout the novel. Its belly 'pulsed with fear', its 'black beady eyes glittering', the rat points forward to the figure Bigger himself will become, the part-real, part-fantasy denizen of a grotesque counter-Darwinian world in which human life—his own, Mary's, Bessie's—seems to evolve backwards into rodent predation and death. Whether in pursuit or the pursued, Bigger becomes damned either way, just as he victimizes others while doubling as both his own and society's victim. These inner meanings of the novel also lie behind Wright's three-part partition of 'Fear', 'Flight' and 'Fate', as much notations of *Native Son*'s parabular meanings as the apparent drama at the surface. Bigger's parting words to Mr. Max suggest that he has some first glimmerings of the process which has metamorphosized him into a human rodent, but he goes to his death still trapped by the predatory laws which he sought to repudiate by throwing the skillet at the rat in the opening chapter.

In 'How Bigger Was Born', Wright speaks of Chicago as 'huge, roaring, dirty, noisy, raw, stark, brutal', that is as the city of the historic stockyards, oppressive Summer humidity and the chill polar winds of the mid-Western Winter. He also speaks of Chicago as a city which has created 'centuries-long chasm[s] of emptiness' in figures like Bigger Thomas. *Native Son* depicts Chicago in just that way: as a literal instance of colour-line urban America but also as the more inward City of Dreadful Night, for Bigger both the world among whose tenements and on whose streets he has been raised and the city which he has internalized, one of violence and half-understood impulses to revenge. To discern in *Native Son* only an urban-realist drama again evades the dimensions of the novel Wright himself knowingly calls 'the whole dark inner landscape of Bigger's mind'.

—A. Robert Lee, "Richard Wright's Inside Narratives," *American Fiction: New Readings*, ed. Richard Gray (New York: Barnes & Noble, 1983), pp. 215–17

❖

JUDITH GIBLIN BRAZINSKY ON THE DRAMATIZATION OF *NATIVE SON*

[Judith Giblin Brazinsky is a former professor of English at the University of South Carolina. In this extract, Brazinsky compares *Native Son* to the dramatization of the novel cowritten by Wright and Paul Green.]

Richard Wright conceived of his novel in dramatic terms. The metaphor of the play appears both in the novel—in which Bigger is called a "hapless actor in this fateful drama"—and in Wright's story of how the novel was written. In "How 'Bigger' Was Born," Wright speaks of his attempt to capture "some insight derived from my living in the form of action, scene, and dialogue." ". . . I wanted the reader to feel that Bigger's story was happening *now,* like a play upon the stage or a movie unfolding upon the screen. . . . Wherever possible, I told of Bigger's life in close-up, slow-motion. . . . I kept out of the story as much as possible, for I wanted the reader to feel there was nothing between him and Bigger; that the story was a special *première* given in his own private theater."

The novel does, in fact, contain many features which enhance its suitability for adaptation to the stage: a limited cast, a strong central character, a tight time frame (the principal action occurring in under thirty-six hours), a clear division into three sections of sustained and powerful action, and a culminatory trial scene. But these features are not those to which Wright's metaphor refers. The novel's other, more important characteristics—the ones Wright describes as dramatic—are, ironically, those characteristics which make its faithful dramatization impossible. Although Wright chose to speak of the relationship between Bigger and the reader as being as immediate and intense as drama staged in a "private theater," it is precisely this psychological intimacy which the theatre—a public experience—cannot duplicate.

Wright demanded of himself and the techniques of the novel the means of compelling a reader to understand and sympathize with a young black man who, in the space of twenty-four hours, accidentally smothers an innocent white woman, decapitates and burns her corpse, attempts to extort $10,000 from her parents, and rapes and murders the black lover he has coerced to help him. These are the chief crimes of Bigger Thomas, but they are by no means the full range of his violence. How so gruesome a plot can be managed with any sympathy for Bigger lies in the brilliance of the narrative method. Tailoring a third-person point of view to encompass stream-of-consciousness and a kind of Jamesian "angle of narration," Wright takes his reader on an intimate psychic odyssey, a voyeuristic journey into the criminal mind. What, in terms of plot, is unrelieved horror becomes bearable only because of the fullness of understanding the reader is permitted, an understanding controlled by Wright's own attitude, conveyed in a sustained tone of sadness which, as Robert A. Bone points out, "emphasizes Bigger's suffering."

There is no comparable combination of techniques in the theatre. Action and dialogue alone are not sufficient to achieve the same effect. Bigger is, in the first place, an inarticulate character who does not understand his own impulses beyond their immediate recognition. Nor can the other characters be said to understand them or be made capable of articulating them as they occur. No matter how expressive an acting talent, the inchoate emotions and half-formed perceptions of a Bigger Thomas are impossible to portray with the same degree of fullness and precision Wright's narrative method permits. As a consequence, Bigger, if brought to the stage, must necessarily be changed. In the absence of mechanisms to exhibit fully his complex though unassimilated emotions, those emotions must inevitably be reduced, simplified, and other methods must be found to elicit audience sympathy. An examination of *Native Son*'s first scene demonstrates these imperatives at work.

Both the novel and the play begin with the ringing of an alarm clock in the cramped one-room kitchenette the four members of the Thomas family share in Chicago's Black Belt. But the similarity quickly ends. In the novel, the alarm wakes Bigger, his brother Buddy, and sister Vera to the equally shrill scolding of an unnamed mother, whose irascibility reflects her strained capacity for coping with their impoverished life. " 'Bigger, shut that thing off!' " she yells. That order is followed by others: " 'Buddy, get up from there!' " " 'Vera! Get up from there! . . . Get up from there, I say.' " Within seconds, their dressing is interrupted by the intrusion of a huge rat, and they are variously galvanized or paralyzed by terror. Bigger's response in killing the rat is a measure of his instinctive fear and rage; he pounds the rat's head with a shoe, "crushing it, cursing hysterically: 'You sonofa*bitch*!' "

The play opens on a different note. The mother, here named Hannah, lovingly admonishes: "You children hurry up. That old clock done struck the half-past." The play both softens and strengthens Bigger's mother, giving her, in addition to a name with Biblical echoes, an essentially optimistic spiritual to sing as she goes about her work in the first moments of the play:

> Jordan River, Chilly and col'
> Chill the body but not the soul—
> Every time I feel the spirit
> Moving in my heart I will pray.

The lyrics contrast with the more secular hymn to hard life and hard work the mother of the novel sings later in the morning:

> *Life is like a mountain railroad*
> *With an engineer that's brave*
> *We must make the run successful*
> *From the cradle to the grave. . . .*

Despite the determination of her son, the mother of the novel is a woman defeated by life, worn down to the raw nerves. In her bitterness and frustration, she lashes out at Bigger: " '. . . sometimes I wonder why I birthed you.' " She laments, " 'All I ever do is try to make a home for you children and you don't care.' "

The Hannah Thomas of the play, in contrast, resembles nothing so much as the stereotypical mammy-figure. She is a sister of Dilsey Gibson, sustained by her religious faith and able to overcome her fear. When in the play Bigger confronts the rat, Hannah Thomas pleads "piteously" for the creature to be spared: "Unstop the hole, let him out." The mother of the novels shrieks, " 'Kill 'im!' "

The killing of the rat is one of the most powerful and revelatory incidents in Wright's plot. Its effect in the novel is to show the terrified helplessness of the Thomas family and Bigger's violent response to his fear. In this, Bigger and the rat are equated, their excessive rage the measure of their terror: "The rat's belly pulsed with fear. Bigger advanced a step and the rat emitted a long thin song of defiance." Before Bigger can kill it, the rat attacks him, leaving a three-inch tear in his trouser leg. Bigger crushes the rat utterly and, in triumphant bravado, flaunts the bloody corpse in his sister's face, enjoying her terror. James Baldwin was among the first to recognize the significance of this episode of fear, rage, and violent action: "One may consider that the entire book . . . is an extension, with the roles inverted, of this chilling metaphor."

—Judith Giblin Brazinsky, "The Demands of Conscience and the Imperatives of Form: The Dramatization of *Native Son,*" *Black American Literature Forum* 18, No. 3 (Fall 1984): 107–8

❖

LOUIS TREMAINE ON BIGGER'S WORLD OF SILENCE

[Louis Tremaine is the translator of Mohammed Dib's *Who Remembers the Sea* (1983) from French into English. In this extract, Tremaine explores Bigger's world of speechlessness and how his lawyer attempts to communicate for him.]

Like the characterization and plot, the narrative voice in *Native Son* serves as more than simply a technical support to a work of fiction. It too functions more particularly as an expressionistic projection of Bigger's sensibility. It not only expresses Bigger's dilemma, but in its particular mode of expression it concretely embodies that dilemma as well.

Broadly speaking, Bigger suffers from an inability to communicate a conscious understanding of his own emotional reality. In a narrower sense, Bigger lacks words and feels this lack as a potent form of alienation from others. James Nagel, commenting on "images of 'vision' in *Native Son*," suggests a similar insight, that only at the end does Bigger realize "that his real tragedy is not death; it is rather the fact of never having been clearly seen by anyone." This is spelled out most clearly when Bigger attempts to express himself to Max, the one person who has come closest to understanding him:

> He could not talk. . . . Max was upon another planet, far off in space. Was there any way to break down this wall of isolation? Distractedly he gazed about the cell, trying to remember where he had heard words that would help him. He could recall none. He had lived outside of the lives of men. Their modes of communication, their symbols and images, had been denied him.

The long-felt need to explain himself becomes at last, in the terms of the plot, a matter of physical survival, for he can finally do nothing to save himself but plead his case to the court, and yet "he knew that the moment he tried to put his feelings into words, his tongue would not move." This premonition proves true when Bigger is given the opportunity to speak in court before being sentenced: "He tried to open his mouth to answer, but could not. Even if he had the power of speech, he did not know what he could have said."

If Bigger cannot speak for himself, however, others can and do speak for him and in the process take from him a large measure of control over his own destiny and over the satisfaction of his own needs. One notices this disparity, for example, when Bigger applies for a job and Mr. and Mrs. Dalton discuss his case in his presence but outside his comprehension: "The long strange words they used made no sense to him; it was another language." The press, often an important pressure impelling the plot forward, is another repository of the power of words, one which Bigger imagines that he has tapped by the power of his own actions:

> The papers ought to be full of him now. It did not seem strange that they should be, for all his life he had felt that things had been happening to him that should have gone into them. But only after he had acted upon feelings which he had had for years would the papers carry the story, *his* story.

The power of the preacher to manipulate, through words, the images that hold meaning for Bigger's life has already been seen. But the most significant figure in this respect, of course, is the lawyer, Max, who promises Bigger, "I'll tell the judge all I can of how you feel and why," and who stands up in court before the assembled representatives of the world Bigger fears but needs, and announces, "*I* shall witness for Bigger Thomas." Max has been characterized by various readers as a mouthpiece for the Communist Party. In fact, he is much more importantly a mouthpiece for Bigger, a fantasy come true: he possesses a vast audience, commands the language (words, imagery, frame of reference) of that audience, and stands in a privileged forum from which to address it. In every sense of the word, he *represents* Bigger to the world in a way that Bigger could never represent himself.

What Max is to Bigger's fictional life, the narrator is to the artistic image that is projected out of that life. The narrator's facility with words and propensity for extended abstract analysis and complex syntax compensate—indeed, *over*-compensate—for Bigger's stance of mute incomprehension before his own experience. As the novel proceeds, Bigger acts and feels while the narrator reasons aloud about these actions and feelings. The relationship is precisely the one described (by the narrator) between the two parts of Bigger as he lies in his cell awaiting trial: "Blind impulses welled up in his body, and his intelligence sought to make them plain to his understanding by supplying images that would explain them." The narrator speaks for Bigger just as Max does, supplying images to his impulses, mind to his body. Max's action is limited, however, and he does not succeed in his effort to explain Bigger. Because he lives in the same external world as Bigger, he faces the same barriers and threats. The "crazy" student in Bigger's cell is another example of someone who tries to express directly his understanding of reality and who suffers as a result. Bigger's only recourse, again, is to imagination, to art. Wright describes, in "How 'Bigger' Was Born," his intention to explain "everything only in terms of Bigger's life and, if possible, in the rhythms of Bigger's thought (even though the words would be mine)," acknowledging readily the range of technical and linguistic devices which contribute to this "explanation," a range which is utterly beyond Bigger's capabilities. And the narrator himself on occasion recognizes the differences between Bigger's voice and his own: "though he could not have put it into words, he felt that . . ." Because Bigger cannot "reach out with his bare hands and carve from naked space the concrete solid reasons" for his actions, the narrator is created to carve those reasons from language, an equally resistant material for Bigger. There is nothing subtle about the narrator of *Native Son:* his comments are obtrusive, overwrought, and tendentious. He lacks sophistication. He is a literary cliché. And he is precisely the narrator Bigger would create, if he were able, to tell his story for him.

—Louis Tremaine, "The Dissociated Sensibility of Bigger Thomas in Wright's *Native Son,*" *Studies in American Fiction* 14, No. 1 (Spring 1986): 73–75

❖

ROBERT JAMES BUTLER ON BIGGER THOMAS AND MARY

[Robert James Butler is the author of Native Son: *The Emergence of a New Black Hero* (1991) and the coeditor of *The City in African American Literature* (1995). In this extract, Butler studies the dual nature of Bigger Thomas, who is by turns "romantic" and "naturalistic" in his relations with Mary.]

This duality in Bigger is even more powerfully revealed in his relationships with Bessie and Mary, who represent the extreme poles of his divided self. Whereas Mary represents a side of

Bigger which may be called "romantic" because it is centered in an idealized set of longings for a radically new life based upon expanded possibilities, Bessie epitomizes an aspect of his personality which may be called "naturalistic" since it is severely conditioned by the economic, political, and social pressures of his actual environment. It is one of the novel's most deeply significant ironies that Bigger is never permitted to relate positively to either woman but is instead driven to destroy them because of his deep-seated fears of what he realizes they represent in him. For one of the more terrifying aspects of his world is that genuine consciousness of self is almost always equated with death: "He knew that the moment he allowed what his life meant to enter fully into his consciousness, he would either kill himself or someone else." In destroying Mary and Bessie, Bigger ironically accomplishes both tasks. For Wright portrays these women not only as separate characters who frustrate Bigger but, more importantly, as externalizations of the extreme limits of his divided self, two poles which he feels compelled to destroy because his world never gives him an opportunity to know, accept, and love them. The net result is not only Bigger's literal death in the electric chair but his own acts of self-destruction, which result in a kind of moral suicide.

Throughout Books One and Two Bigger and Mary are subtly linked, even though they appear to come from separate universes. Both characters are alienated from their environments and are perceived as aberrant by many of the people who are closest to them. In the novel's opening scene, Bigger's mother becomes so exasperated by his behavior that she calls him " 'crazy' " and warns him about the direction his life is taking: " 'You'll regret how you living some day. . . . If you don't stop running with that gang of yours and do right you'll end up where you never thought you would.' " In the same way, Peggy, the Daltons' maid, characterizes Mary as " 'kind of wild,' " a well-intentioned but naive girl who worries her folks " 'to death' " by running around with " 'a wild and crazy bunch of reds.' " Just as Mrs. Thomas views her son's erratic behavior as a threat to the well-being of their family, Peggy claims that Mary's activities run counter to order and stability in the family: " 'If it wasn't for Mary and her wild ways, this household would run like a clock.' " To further reinforce these similarities between the two characters, Mr. Dalton describes Mary as " 'that crazy daughter of mine' " directly after he has characterized Bigger as a sort of " 'problem boy.' "

What Wright suggests here by these important parallels is that Bigger and Mary share a common humanity, despite the obvious dissimilarities arising from their radically different social and economic backgrounds. Although this humanity is frustrated in different ways by environment, the same results are produced: alienation and rebellion. Mary's physically comfortable life has given her privileges and opportunities denied to Bigger, but it has also stunted her growth by making her "blind" to reality. Just as Bigger has been walled off from many aspects of life by his stark poverty and his status as a black man in a white world, Mary has been separated from real experience by overly protective parents and her privileged status as a rich white girl. Both respond to their situations in very similar ways—Bigger in forming a gang which engages in acts of rebellion by robbing stores, and Mary by developing friendships with Communists who are committed to overturning society by redistributing wealth. Both characters rebel strongly against the families into which they are born because they sense that these families block their own human development. Because Bigger is "sick of his life at home" he becomes part of a peer group that represents everything of which his mother does not approve. Mary too feels stifled by the limits imposed upon her by her family and deliberately opposes their wishes by running away to New York, taking off with Jan to Florida, and entering his circle of radicals.

On a more basic level, the common humanity shared by Bigger and Mary is dramatized by their strong sexual attraction to each other. Mary, who wants to know more about the rougher aspects of life from which she has been protected, is romantically attracted to Bigger, just as he is drawn to her apparently glamorous life because it represents a world of pleasure and possibility from which he has been excluded and which he has seen only in movies. From the beginning, Bigger connects Mary with the film he has seen which gives a romantic view of rich white women who will " 'do anything.' " Such films fill him with a sense of excitement because they evoke a sense of possibility which is a natural part of his character that has been frustrated by environment. Linking his perception of the movie with a remembered story of a white woman who has actually married her chauffeur, he goes to work for the Daltons with a sense that the job might contain "'something *big*'" for him. Although he is not consciously aware of it, he has made a number of assumptions about Mary even before he has met her: She symbolizes a world for which a substantial part of himself has been longing, and he feels that this world may be reachable through sex.

> —Robert James Butler, "The Function of Violence in Richard Wright's *Native Son*," *Black American Literature Forum* 20, Nos. 1–2 (Spring–Summer 1986): 11–13

❖

JOYCE ANN JOYCE ON MAX AND THE COMMUNIST PARTY

[Joyce Ann Joyce (b. 1949) is Lincoln Professor of English at the University of Maryland. She has written *Warriors, Conjurers and Priests: Defining African Centered Literary Criticism* (1994) and coedited *The New Cavalcade: African American Writing from 1760 to the Present* (1991–92). In this extract from *Richard Wright's Art of Tragedy* (1986), Joyce explores the significance of Bigger Thomas's lawyer and the Communist party in *Native Son*.]

Max, of course, does not defend Bigger because of a genuine concern for him as an individual human being. When Max encounters Buckley in the room where Bigger is being held, Max reveals his self-serving political purpose for defending Bigger as he accuses Buckley of defaming the Communist party. Because Buckley takes advantage of Bigger's having falsified the Communist insignia on the kidnap note, Max's party compels him to defend Bigger in an attempt to correct the slurs against it and to mitigate the harassment of party members, as well as to advance their cause. In contrast to the plethora of witnesses for the state—Mrs. Dalton, her mother, Britten, fifteen newspapermen, five handwriting specialists, a fingerprint expert, six doctors, four waitresses from Ernie's Kitchen Shack, two white schoolteachers, Jan, the members of Bigger's gang, Doc, and five psychiatrists—Max chooses to be the sole witness for the defense.

In his pretrial statement, Max introduces the ideas on which he later builds his plea to the judge. He urges the judge to remember that the law of the state offers three choices regarding a plea of guilty in a murder case: "the court may impose the death penalty, imprison the defendant for life, or for a term of not less than fourteen years." He explains that this law allows the court the flexibility to consider why a man killed and to use its findings either to aggravate or mitigate the measure of punishment. Pointing out that in its pretrial statement the state has dismissed the issue of why Bigger killed, Max ends his introduction with the ideas that dominate his subsequent address: his tasks will be to elucidate the reasons why Bigger's crimes are "almost instinctive" by nature and to convince the judge that since Bigger's motives are not included in the laws as they are written, he must consider Bigger's mental and emotional makeup before deciding his punishment.

As soon as Max begins his address proper, the reader quickly perceives that such a plea as his will be futile in counteracting the power of the forces that demand Bigger's life. If the nature and length of Max's address frustrate the reader, it is not difficult to imagine the judge's response and that of the others in the courtroom. In contrast to Buckley's well-timed, sensational, vitriolic performance, Max's excessively long speech challenges the intellectual and moral faculties of the observers. In his pretrial statement Buckley quite aptly characterizes Max's speech and presages its effect when he says, "There is no room here for evasive, theoretical, or fanciful interpretations of the law."

Interweaving the image patterns, Bigger's personality, and the elements of setting into the fabric of the speech, Wright has Max give a theoretical interpretation of what it means to be Bigger Thomas. Wright has him echo both the ironic title of the novel and the elements of setting at the very beginning, when Max pronounces that Bigger's destiny is America's destiny. As implied by the title of the novel, Bigger is a creation of an

American culture that ironically rejects him and denies his social, economic, and political freedom. This denial, Max avers, has a crippling effect on those who control Bigger's life as well as on Bigger. Max's idea that the white world's life and fate are linked to Bigger's parallels Wright's use of *black* and *white* as well as the images of the snow and the sun. The symbolic meanings of *black* and *white* reflect the contrast in Bigger's and Mary's emotional makeup and underline the relationship that describes their lives. For while the white characters define themselves in relation to the Black, the Blacks in turn depend on the whites for their social, political, and economic livelihood. Also a part of Wright's depiction of this relationship, the snow and the sun represent respectively the white world's power and hostility and Bigger's reaction to that power.

Max's address directly attributes Bigger's rebelliousness and fear to the godlike power the Daltons have over Bigger and his kind. Synonymous with the "white looming mountain" and the image of the wall (see Chapter 4), various sections of Max's speech show how the social and economic barriers that separate the black and white worlds are so great that they have the same power and psychological effect on Bigger as acts of nature. Max says: "When situations like this arise, instead of men feeling that they are facing other men, they feel that they are facing mountains, floods, seas: forces of nature whose size and strength focus the minds and emotions to a degree of tension unusual in the quiet routine of urban life. Yet this tension exists within the limits of urban life, undermining it and supporting it in the same gesture of being."

This tension between the alluring and repellent aspects of urban culture contains a double-barreled irony. Illuminating a part of this irony, Max paints an esoteric picture of the forbidden fruits that taunt Bigger:

> Your Honor, consider the mere physical aspect of our civilization. How alluring, how dazzling it is! How it excites the senses! How it seems to dangle within easy reach of everyone the fulfillment of happiness! How constantly and overwhelmingly the advertisements, radios, newspapers and movies play upon us! But in thinking of them remember that to many they are tokens of mockery. . . . Imagine a man walking amid such a scene, a part of it, and yet knowing that it is *not* for him!

Reminiscent of the setting of Books 1 and 2—which contrasts Bigger's thwarted aspirations and the poverty of his home environment with Mary's unfettered lifestyle and the luxuries of her home environment—Max's portrait presents the paradox reflected in the environmental constituents that affect Bigger's consciousness.

—Joyce Ann Joyce, *Richard Wright's Art of Tragedy* (Iowa City: University of Iowa Press, 1986), pp. 103–6

❖

LAURA E. TANNER ON LANGUAGE IN *NATIVE SON*

[Laura E. Tanner (b. 1961) is the author of *Intimate Violence: Reading Rape and Torture in Twentieth-Century Fiction* (1994). In this extract, Tanner discusses Bigger Thomas's difficulties in expressing himself and the function of language in *Native Son*.]

Through the narrator's comments, we are forced to read both the text of Bigger's actions and the interpretive gloss that leads us away from the material substance of those actions into a symbolic universe in which they are reinscribed within the narrator's own language game. The narrator equates Bigger's act of murder with the creation of a universe in which Bigger's existence is governed not by the alien world view forced upon him by whites but by a reality of his own making. Ironically, however, it is the narrator's depiction of Bigger's murder as an attempt to achieve stable linguistic referentiality that exposes most clearly the radical instability of language. The clash between the literal and symbolic portrayal of Bigger's existence emphasizes for the reader the very problem that the narrator exposes: the capacity for distortion inherent in the mode of representation. Even as the narrator uses Bigger's character to comment on the necessity of demystifying language, the narrative itself participates in the kind of unauthorized "symbolic and psychological justification" against which Ellison warns.

Although the narrator's observations are clothed in layers of abstract, metaphorical language, recent critics have had no difficulty in accepting those observations as the straightforward articulation of Bigger's thoughts. In the passages where Bigger's thoughts are actually transcribed rather than translated, however, the distortion inherent in the narrator's rendering of those thoughts is fully apparent. The introduction of Bigger's language is usually signaled by a sudden shift to the short, choppy sentences that characterize his awkward relationship with the master language. Where the narrator's voice is defined by a smooth-flowing prose style that relies upon the complex use of balance and antithesis, compound constructions, and periodic sentences, Bigger's voice is marked by a form of halting expression that frequently deteriorates into stuttering repetition. Bigger's uncultivated speech is often framed by the imagistic, lyrical voice of the narrator:

> He stared at the furnace. He trembled with another idea. He—he could, he—he could put her in the furnace. He would burn her! That was the safest thing of all to do. He went to the furnace and opened the door. A huge red bed of coals blazed and quivered with molten fury.

It is only in juxtaposition with the final sentence of this passage that the awkward diction and hesitant articulation of the lines preceding that sentence are revealed to the reader in all their clumsiness. Unlike the earlier sentences, the final sentence—with its internal rhyme, alliteration, and controlled imagery—has an ease and facility with language that expresses its author's relaxed association with words.

Bigger's awkward relationship to written language is expressed most clearly in his composition of the kidnap note. In the passage describing Bigger's act of creation, the narrative assumes his voice; the crude diction and phrasing of the note is uncomfortably emphasized by the linguistic deterioration of the narrative itself:

> He swallowed with dry throat. Now, what would be the best kind of note? He thought, I want you to put ten thousand . . . Naw; that would not do. Not "I." It would be better to say "we." We got your daughter, he printed slowly in big round letters. That was better. . . . Now, tell him not to go to the police. Don't

go to the police if you want your daughter back safe. Naw; that ain't good.

Bigger's painful relationship with the master language assaults the reader's ear as s/he hears the broken English of Bigger's kidnap note reflected in the dissonant tones of the narrative itself. The sudden intrusion of the narrator's voice that follows may be an attempt to "translate" Bigger's feelings into the sophisticated prose to which he has no access; in fact, however, the narrator's intrusion wrests the pen from Bigger's hand and undercuts any authority he might have had: "His scalp tingled with excitement; it seemed that he could feel each strand of hair upon his head. . . . There was in his stomach a slow, cold, vast rising movement, as though he held within the embrace of his bowels the swing of planets through space." The magnitude of the narrator's metaphorical vehicle and his skillful control of language contrast painfully with the limited scope of Bigger's action and the unsophisticated way in which he uses words; thus, the passage actually subverts Bigger's authority while appearing to validate it.

The tension between narrative voice and subject exposed here erupts in a condescending tone that verges on racist objectification at several points in the novel. The narrator's command of language allows him an excuse for the generalizations he makes about Bigger; in lending a voice to those less articulate than himself, he exposes the prejudices of the language game through which he speaks: "To Bigger and his kind white people were not really people; they were a sort of great natural force, like a stormy sky looming overhead, or like a deep swirling river stretching suddenly at one's feet in the dark . . . whether they feared it or not, each and every day of their lives they lived with it; even when words did not sound its name, they acknowledged its reality." Whomever "Bigger and his kind" may be, it is clear that they do not partake of the narrator's superior vision or capacity for self-expression; their wordlessness creates a vacuum in which he can construct a reality which their silence is said to affirm. Neither his poetic alliteration nor his imagistic description of that reality, however, can disguise the fact that the narrator's vision relies upon a generalized notion of Bigger that is dangerously limited. In his eagerness to speak for "Bigger and his kind," the narrator inadvertently discloses his own narrow understanding of Bigger's identity: "But maybe it would never come; maybe there was no such thing for him; maybe he would have to go to his end just as he was, dumb, driven, with the shadow of emptiness in his eyes." Is it really Bigger who alternates between considering himself the sophisticated reader of his own actions and the brute defined by existential emptiness? Both assessments would seem to indicate conversely exaggerated and objectified "readings" of Bigger's existence; the character who holds "in the embrace of his bowels the swing of planets through space" and his counterpart, the "dumb" and "driven" murderer, are both narrative creations born of symbolic language and abstract analysis.

—Laura E. Tanner, "Uncovering the Magical Disguise of Language: The Narrative Presence in Richard Wright's *Native Son*," *Texas Studies in Literature and Language* 29, No. 4 (Winter 1987): 414–16

❖

ALAN W. FRANCE ON MISOGYNY IN *NATIVE SON*

[Alan W. France is a professor of English at West Chester University (West Chester, Pennsylvania). In this extract, written when he was a graduate student at Texas Christian University, France condemns the misogyny that he sees as both literally and symbolically expressed in *Native Son*.]

Even feminist critics of Wright's work, while noting its strains of violence and misogyny, have not opened the text sufficiently to reveal its submerged underside. Sherley Anne Williams, for example, observes Wright's tendency to portray black women as treacherous and traitorous and to present their suffering as, primarily, "an affront to the masculinity of black men." Williams, nevertheless, fails to challenge Wright's authority over the interpretation of female characters in *Native Son:* "We excuse these characterizations [of women]," she writes, "because of the power of Wright's psychological portrait of

Bigger; this is Bigger's story." It is time now to revoke these privileges accorded to Bigger and to recover the radical alterity in the text that reduces women to property, valuable only to the extent they serve as objects of phallocentric status conflicts. If read as the negative polarity of the text, this process of male reification and appropriation pervades the work.

In the initial episode of *Native Son*, Bigger kills a huge rat while his mother and sister, Vera, cower and scream on the bed in fear. This emblematic act occupies the surface of the novel's first six pages. The rat, an omnivorous, disease-bearing pest, fairly represents the socioeconomic system under which Mr. Dalton squeezes his fortune out of the ghetto. The killing of the rat represents, perhaps, Bigger's one chance to protect his mother and younger siblings as the patriarch of the Thomas family. The text urges us specifically to make this latter interpretation when its omniscient narrator tells us:

> He [Bigger] hated his family because he knew that they were suffering and that he was powerless to help them. He knew that the moment he allowed himself to feel to its fullness how they lived, the shame and misery of their lives, he would be swept out of himself with fear and despair.

In this passage we are asked to privilege Bigger Thomas' feeling of powerlessness caused by the family's living conditions over the actual physical suffering that those conditions impose on the family. The text, that is, points to Bigger's status deprivation as the real significance of economic and social oppression.

In this initial episode, Bigger experiences his killing of the rat not with the pride of one who alleviates his family's distress, if only partially and temporarily, but with the giddy exultation of one glorying in the rare and momentary dominance that killing an adversary confers. Bigger uses the occasion of conquest to lord it over the dependent females of his family.

The phallocentricity of this scene is created first of all by Bigger's threatening his sister with the crushed and bloody carcass of the rat. The threat to Bigger (and the phallic suggestiveness can here be noted in his name) is indicated by a suggestively vaginal "three-inch rip" in his pant-leg. Bigger crushes the rat's head with his shoe while "cursing hysterically:

You sonofa*bitch!*" The italics further suggest a reading of the episode as a struggle for phallic dominance with overtones of castration anxiety. In the economy of male aggression, Bigger's killing of the rat converts it into an object "over a foot long" that now becomes a weapon in his hands. As victor in a battle that the text compels us to see In overtly sexual terms, Bigger attempts to exact the maximum abasement of those whose subordination he has won by right of conquest. When Vera begs him to throw the rat out, "Bigger laughed and approached the bed with the dangling rat, swinging it to and fro like a pendulum, enjoying his sister's fear." It is not the conquest over the rat, *qua* rat, in which Bigger most exults. Rather, he enjoys the dominance over the women that violent conquest has conferred on him.

Nor is it merely the physical destruction of the rat—its reduction to symbolic phallus—that allows him dominance over the women: it is their own contemptible weakness, that which denies them utterance of the words of the novel's epitaph from Job: "My stroke is heavier than my groaning." From the very beginning of the text, narrative instructions make clear that the absent phallus is the source of shame as well as weakness. The mother calls to the sons as she stands in her nightgown in the single-room apartment, "Turn your heads so I can dress." Bigger and his brother, Buddy, "kept their faces averted while their mother and sister put on enough clothes to keep them from feeling ashamed. . . ." And this aversion of the eyes is "a conspiracy against shame." From the very outset of the novel, therefore, the text's psychodynamics are polarized sexually: Bigger and other male characters continue the violent struggle, presaged by the killing of the rat, for the appropriation or continued enjoyment of—the narcissistic desire for—status. Women, as characters in *Native Son,* are objects of this appropriation; they are at the same time desired as objects but contemptible in their weakness and passivity.

The woman, as displaced Other, is characterized as blind and weak. Mrs. Dalton is literally sightless; but to Bigger, all the characters who are not conscious of the predatory economy in which they are immersed are blind. It is, in fact, the killing of Mary Dalton that makes Bigger aware of the general blindness. After Mary's murder, he notices that those around him "did not want to see what others were doing if that doing did not feed their own desires." The corollary is that "if he could see while the others were blind, then he could get what he wanted and never be caught at it." Mrs. Thomas' religion and Bessie's drinking blind and weaken these women, arousing Bigger's abhorrence: "He hated his mother for that way of hers which was like Bessie's. What his mother had was Bessie's whiskey, and Bessie's whiskey was his mother's religion."

—Alan W. France, "Misogyny and Appropriation in Wright's *Native Son*," *Modern Fiction Studies* 34, No. 3 (Autumn 1988): 414–16

❖

EUGENE E. MILLER ON SURREALISM IN *NATIVE SON*

[Eugene E. Miller is the author of *Voice of a Native Son: The Poetics of Richard Wright* (1990), from which the following extract is taken. Here, Miller explores the influence of French Surrealism on *Native Son*.]

In terms of his own techniques, what of Surrealism that seems most obviously to have impressed Wright was the "wakeful dream," a state cultivated in artistic production by Surrealists and an aura that pervades many of their works, which employ realistic details or technique but in overall contexts that give them a quality associated with dreams.

This condition is very evident in the *Native Son* scenes depicting Bigger's initiation into the Dalton's world:

> He would see in a few moments if the Daltons . . . were like the people he had seen and heard in the movie. But while walking through the quiet and spacious white neighborhood, he did not feel the pull and mystery of the thing as he had in the movies. . . . The houses he passed were huge; lights glowed softly in the windows. The streets were empty, save for an occasional car that zoomed past on swift rubber tires. This was a cold and distant world; a world of white secrets carefully guarded.

He looked around the room; it was lit by dim lights glowing from a hidden source. He tried to find them by roving his eyes, but could not. . . . On the smooth walls were several paintings whose nature he tried to make out, but failed . . . a faint sound of piano music floated to him from somewhere. He was sitting in a white house; dim lights burned around him; strange objects challenged him.

Bigger listened, blinking and bewildered. The long strange words they used made no sense to him. . . . He felt from the tone of their voices that they were having a difference of opinion about him, but he could not determine what it was about. It made him uneasy, tense, as though there were influences and presences about him which he could feel but not see.

The eerie disquietude that eminates from these scenes is not unlike the spirit that irradiates many Surrealist paintings. In the first excerpt cited above, the absence of people, the deserted streets suggesting empty distances of planes converging to a vanishing point, the oversized buildings, the "zoom" that stresses the silence, the phrase "swift rubber tires" suggesting free-roaming circles—all disembodied from the usual components—recall the Surrealist work of Chirico. All of these scenes suggest a world of indeterminacy, an untethering of ordinary objects—the houses, the piano music, the lights, the language, Bigger himself—by stripping away their usual significations and placing them in a foreign context. This practice gives rise to an emotional equivalent of what the Surrealists often spoke of as their objective—a conscious, awake-dream state of perception.

All of Native Son, in addition to depicting Bigger's descent into and movement through an unknown, the terrifying yet exhilarating exterior white world that is so rich and full of significance (value, meaning) that it is also not what it appears and hence is unpredictable, filled with chance—with opportunity and hazard—also depicts Bigger's journey through the depths of his unknown self, through a maelstrom into a sense of self that offers to cancel out the antinomies that conventional modes of apprehending reality have told him exist between himself and the rest of the world. While he has only a glimmer of this kind of unification, he has approached it, and there is a sufficient unification of self, within himself and in his relationship with the outside world, that Wright can have him exclaim,

"What I killed for, *I am!*" By having Bigger utter and apply to himself the biblical name that God gave to Himself, Wright makes us see Bigger as a deified human; as deified, he is a being who somehow encompasses all, however deformed his external image may appear. In Surrealism, this all is achieved when one approaches the "supreme point." Wright, like Breton, has not only secularized the "point of origin for the Creation, and the point of action at which God created the world and at which all is contained *ab ovo*" (Carrouges, *André Breton and the Basic Concepts of Surrealism*), but, as Alquié says Breton also did, Wright has psychologized it, placing it with the subjective, cognitive emotions and developing the consciousness of Bigger. The metaphysical dimension, so emaciated in modern Western civilization, is thus supplied by the very mind that requires it.

Wright's own sense of the novel's surrealistic quality is particularly revealed in the film he made of the book in 1949–50. He may not have sought the acquaintance of French Surrealists, but he is credited with having introduced into the film version one of its more successful features, one that shows the claim Surrealism still had on his imagination. Near the end of the film, in many ways its high point, Bigger's emotional state is recapitulated not through the rather static device of Max's courtroom oral presentation but by means of a dream sequence. Set designs include the Dalton basement that is transformed into something definitely out of the Surrealist paintings by Chirico and Dali. During the action, Bigger does not reach for a stick that becomes a serpent; he does reach out for a figure that appears to be his father but turns into the menacing police chief, and Mary Dalton's severed head (blond in the black and white movie) is merged with bolls of cotton in a huge field. The surrealist quality of the novel is perhaps further attested by the most recent film version. While not so obviously, it too preserves visual effects reminiscent of Surrealist paintings: wide-angle shots, scenes of sparsely furnished rooms with open foregrounds, suggestive of isolated individuals moving about in a dream-like environment.

However, it was, Wright says in the memoir, the composition of the original versions *The Man Who Lived Underground,* not *Native Son,* that brought together and incorporated most successfully in "contour" his grandmother's and the Afro-American folk's mentality, a pattern of thought parallel to the essence of what Stein's prose and Surrealism helped him realize was capturable in a secular, artistic, modern aesthetic form. That story, then, never published in its original length, needs to be investigated in order to see just what Wright had produced that he felt best fulfilled, up to that time, his own poetics. That story, even more pronouncedly than Burke had observed of *Native Son,* employs the Surrealist technique of juxtaposing disparate items.

> —Eugene E. Miller, *Voice of a Native Son: The Poetics of Richard Wright* (Jackson: University of Mississippi Press, 1990), pp. 91–94

❖

JEAN-FRANÇOIS GOUNARD ON EXISTENTIALISM IN *NATIVE SON*

[Jean-François Gounard, a French literary critic, has written *The Racial Problem in the Works of Richard Wright and James Baldwin* (1992), from which the following extract is taken. Here, Gounard examines book three of *Native Son* and compares the existential aspects of the novel to Albert Camus's *The Stranger.*]

If Book Three of the novel lacks the dramatic intensity of the first two books, it nonetheless enables Wright to describe the action in a period of time that lends itself to his ideas. From the moment of his arrest, Bigger is caught up in the gears of a racist justice that wants only his death. Wright accurately depicts the important moments of this legal action: a mere eleven days elapse between the young black man's arrest and his condemnation to death, set for Friday, March 3. Three days after his capture, on Thursday afternoon, Bigger attends the judicial inquiry. He is then taken to the Daltons' for a recreation of the crime and is finally locked away in the Chicago Central Prison. The next day his indictment takes place. It is decided that his trial is to open three days later. The trial takes place at the Criminal Court of Chicago. After three days, Bigger Thomas is condemned to die in the electric chair. A few days later, the young black man will no longer be of this world.

In order to plunge Book Three into an atmosphere as real as that of the first two books, Wright shows the extent to which a single black man can affect the lives of millions of whites. Since he fears serious social problems, the mayor of Chicago encourages the police to step up their vigilance. During Bigger's trial the governor of Illinois calls on the help of two regiments of reservists to guard the court and the Central Prison. The young black man's trial takes place in an extremely tense political and social atmosphere. Bigger appears as a social symbol void of any human conscience. He represents modern man. Margaret Just Butcher thinks that Communism is uncalled for and that it hampers the development of the novel. This black American woman finds it unpleasant that Wright's Marxism denounces the wrongs of American society. Numerous American critics feel, like her, that Wright could have attained the same goal without using Communist ideology. But in 1940, Marxist ideology was practically the only means by which the American black could express his thoughts and his desires.

Wright thus enables Bigger Thomas to confront, alone, a society that denies him human value. This young black man goes into action to attract the attention of those around him and to prove his existence to eyes until then blind. Bigger Thomas's conduct shows that, for the first time in his works known in 1940, Wright had clearly formulated certain fundamental elements of existentialism. In *Richard Wright,* Robert Bone underlines the fact that, "Having rejected Christianity and Communism, Bigger finds the strength to die in the courageous acceptance of his existential self." When he says, "What I killed for, *I am!*" The hero of *Native Son* is, in his own way, an existentialist. In his philosophical essay *L'Existentialisme est un humanisme,* Jean-Paul Sartre says, "Man is constantly outside of himself; it is by projecting himself and by losing himself outside of himself that he makes man exist and, on the other hand, it is by pursuing transcendent goals that he can exist." Bigger's symbolic action is taken in the name of the twelve million blacks who were living in America in 1940. To use Sartre's terms, Bigger projects himself, loses himself outside of himself, in order to establish the human value of the man of color.

Thanks to his act and especially to the privileged position he holds in the eyes of the oppressed blacks, the hero of *Native Son* becomes the symbol and the hope of a race that has never ceased to struggle. The essential aim of this struggle has always been to create a human identity respected by all ethnic and racial groups who form the framework of American society. Bigger becomes the center of a question that preoccupies black America.

One should not think that Bigger's action is that of the ordinary black. It is that of the young black man who has become aware of his freedom and of his acts. He acts with the sole aim of creating an identity for himself. He knows that he will be what he does. The future of his life will depend on the way he conducts himself. It is only through his action that the young black man shows his brothers of color the road to follow.

Even after having learned of his condemnation to death, Bigger has the profound feeling of having accomplished something important for himself and his race. Wright accentuates the isolation and lack of understanding surrounding his act and the hero himself: Bigger only trusts himself. Here Wright explains an idea later developed by Sartre, who says, "Man must find himself again himself and convince himself that nothing can save him from himself." Man is always alone and can count on no one. Blacks and whites in Chicago reject Bigger's act and do not understand its symbolic significance.

The accidental murder committed by Bigger Thomas strangely resembles what happens to the man of whom Albert Camus speaks in *L'Étranger*. Meursault becomes a murderer because of a beach, an Arab, some sunlight, and a revolver. He kills the Arab following a combination of fortuitous circumstances. Bigger Thomas smothers Mary Dalton by instinct, to avoid being discovered in the room of a white woman. Panic-stricken, he can no longer control his acts.

There is, however, a fundamental difference between Meursault and Bigger. Each of them adopts a different attitude towards the world after the crime. The young Frenchman shows only indifference towards everything around him. The young American becomes aware of his human value after having accepted the consequences of his act. Meursault invites one to think of the world in terms of absurdity, life in terms of despair, whereas Bigger gives life a positive meaning.

A few days after the publication of *Native Son*, Wright drafted the text of a lecture he gave at the Schomburg Collection in Harlem. The black audience permitted him to express freely his views on the manner in which he had conceived the novel. That essay "How 'Bigger' Was Born" gives *Native Son* a complex meaning. If in it Wright relates certain events of his youth which influenced the composition of the novel, he wishes above all to show that there is a close relationship between real life and the imaginative work. Disappointed after seeing some bankers' daughters weeping on the pages of *Uncle Tom's Children: Four Novellas,* Wright had decided to reveal the reality of the black world. His aim was to make that reality as harsh and as violent as possible so as to prevent any person from getting over the plight of blacks by shedding some comforting tears. *Native Son* was the result.

—Jean-François Gounard, *The Racial Problem in the Works of Richard Wright and James Baldwin,* tr. Joseph J. Rodgers, Jr. (Westport, CT: Greenwood Press, 1992), pp. 75–77

❖

JAMES CAMPBELL ON RICHARD WRIGHT IN PARIS

[James Campbell (b. 1951) has written *Talking at the Gates: A Life of James Baldwin* (1991) and *Exiled in Paris: Richard Wright, James Baldwin, Samuel Beckett and Others on the Left Bank* (1995). In this extract, Campbell investigates the impact of Richard Wright's days in Paris on his development as a novelist.]

Unlike the tourists who peeped round the classically proportioned pillars of the Café de Flore, Wright read his Sartre—but slowly, and piecemeal. *L'Etre et le néant ⟨Being and Nothingness⟩* was not yet translated into English, and in any case its great philosophical universe was difficult to encompass for someone not trained in its conceptual vocabulary. The long essay 'Anti-Semite and Jew' was published in *Partisan Review* in 1946; he read that, and the lecture 'Existentialism and Humanism', a summary of the themes of *Being and Nothingness,* which came out in English the following year. One of Sartre's themes was that alienation, self-mutilation, the inauthenticity of the individual, grew out of the individual's acceptance of the social labels used to define him: Jew or Aryan, even ugly or handsome. In 'Existentialism and Humanism', Sartre declared that 'Man is nothing else but what he makes of himself. . . . Man is condemned to be free in his choice of action. He is doomed to bear the burden of responsibility.'

Those words made sense to Richard Wright. But, he argued with Sartre when they met, from where he stood the attempt to choose to be something other than what society had determined for you, might be fatal. What use was 'choice' if it led to a lynching? In America, the Negro who 'chose' freedom was fundamentally no more free than the Negro who chose to dwell in the forms of obsequious submission to which society had directed him. The latter was trapped by a social tyranny; the former was trapped by the knowledge that his choice might bring persecution or death.

This was the problem Wright had tackled in his novel *Native Son,* the story of a black youth in Chicago who takes a job as chauffeur to a rich liberal family. On his first night, after carrying home the drunken daughter who has been flirting with him, he smothers her with a pillow, in order to avoid being discovered in her bedroom. Wright had not read any Sartre at the time of writing his novel, but his purpose was 'Sartrean' enough, to explore which ways to freedom were open to his hero:

> Having been thrown by an accidental murder into a position where he had sensed a possible order and meaning in his relations with the people about him; having accepted the moral guilt and responsibility for that murder because it had made him feel free for the first time in his life . . . he chose not to struggle any more.

This is Wright in the act of formulating an 'existentialism'— without at the time having the word in his vocabulary—of the black American mind. Where Sartre's decision to choose freedom led to freedom itself, for Bigger Thomas it led to the electric chair.

Contemplation of the example of Richard Wright would eventually contribute to a change in direction in Sartre's thinking, as he began to focus more on the colonial, rather than the proletarian, as the victim of capitalist oppression. He devoted several pages to the American author in the essays he was currently writing for *Les Temps Modernes,* which would later be published as *Qu'est-ce que c'est la littérature?* (*What Is Literature?*). And Wright drew on the rich fund of Sartre's ideas, which in Paris were in the air, part of the atmosphere of every café and salon, for the novel he started work on soon after his arrival.

As he dwelt on Sartre's ideas, there occurred a shift in the way Wright actually began to experience himself. When he went to Paris he made a discovery, which was that *Angst* did not begin and end with the fact of being a Negro. The condition of the outsider had dimensions he had never previously had cause, or even opportunity, to explore. *Angst* was not spelled b-l-a-c-k. Until now, colour itself had stood between him and this discovery. The realization made him feel like a man and not a 'black man'. Paris and Sartre revealed this to Richard Wright; as a revelation, it meant a great deal more than witnessing at first hand the famous sites of the Lost Generation. This was why he came to Paris—not to walk gaily up the rue Cardinal Lemoine sniffing the footprints of Hemingway. Paris seemed to endow all its visitors with the ease of gesture that refreshed the whole person, a freedom of expression that surprised and renewed the speaker—whether an artist of the last century or a tourist stepping off the boat in 1946. But the freedom it gave Richard Wright was distinct, and he would describe it in poetic rather than philosophical terms: all his life he had felt as if he was carrying a corpse around with him; when he came to Paris, he felt the corpse slipping off his back.

—James Campbell, *Paris Interzone: Richard Wright, Lolita, Boris Vian and Others on the Left Bank 1946–1960* (London: Secker & Warburg, 1994), pp. 11–13

❖

Works by
Richard Wright

Uncle Tom's Children: Four Novellas. 1938, 1940 (as *Uncle Tom's Children: Five Long Stories*).

Bright and Morning Star. 1938.

Native Son. 1940.

How "Bigger" Was Born: The Story of Native Son, *One of the Most Significant Novels of Our Time, and How It Came to Be Written.* 1940.

Native Son (The Biography of a Young American) (drama; with Paul Green). 1941.

The Negro and Parkway Community House. 1941.

12 Million Black Voices: A Folk History of the Negro in the United States. 1941.

Black Boy: A Record of Childhood and Youth. 1945.

A Hitherto Unpublished Manuscript by Richard Wright: Being a Continuation of Black Boy. c. 1946.

The F B Eye Blues. 1949.

The Outsider. 1953.

Savage Holiday. 1954.

Black Power: A Record of Reactions in a Land of Pathos. 1954.

The Color Curtain: A Report on the Bandung Conference. 1956.

The Pagan Spain. 1956.

White Man, Listen! 1957.

The Long Dream. 1958.

Eight Men. 1961.

Lawd Today. 1963.

Letters to Joe C. Brown. Ed. Thomas Knipp. 1968.

The Man Who Lived Underground. Ed. Michel Febre, tr. Claude Emonde Magny. 1971.

American Hunger. 1977.

Richard Wright Reader. Ed. Ellen Wright and Michel Fabre. 1978.

⟨*Works.*⟩ 1991. 2 vols.

Works about Richard Wright and Native Son

Avery, Evelyn Gross. *Rebels and Victims: The Fiction of Richard Wright and Bernard Malamud.* Port Washington, NY: Kennikat Press, 1979.

Baker, Houston A., Jr. "Racial Wisdom and Richard Wright's *Native Son.*" In Baker's *Long Black Song: Essays in Black American Literature and Culture.* Charlottesville: University Press of Virginia, 1972, pp. 122–41.

Bell, Bernard W. *The Afro-American Novel and Its Tradition.* Amherst: University of Massachusetts Press, 1987.

Benston, Kimberly W. "The Veil of Black: (Un)Masking the Subject of African-American Modernism's 'Native Son.' " *Human Studies* 16 (1993): 69–99.

Blake, Caesar R. "On *Native Son.*" In *Rough Justice: Essays on Crime in Literature,* ed. M. L. Friedland. Toronto: University of Toronto Press, 1991, pp. 187–99.

Bloom, Harold, ed. *Bigger Thomas.* New York: Chelsea House, 1990.

———. *Richard Wright.* New York: Chelsea House, 1987.

———, ed. *Richard Wright's* Native Son. New York: Chelsea House, 1988.

Brignano, Russell C. *Richard Wright: An Introduction to the Man and His Works.* Pittsburgh: University of Pittsburgh Press, 1970.

Bryant, Jerry H. "The Violence of *Native Son.*" *Southern Review* 17 (1981): 303–19.

Butler, Robert. Native Son: *The Emergence of a New Black Hero.* Boston: Twayne, 1991.

Cobb, Nina Kressner. "Richard Wright: Exile and Existentialism." *Phylon* 40 (1979): 362–74.

————. "Richard Wright: Individualism Reconsidered." *CLA Journal* 21 (1978): 335–54.

De Arman, Charles. "Bigger Thomas: The Symbolic Negro and the Discrete Human Entity." *Black American Literature Forum* 12 (1978): 61–64.

Fabre, Michel. *Richard Wright: Books and Writers.* Jackson: University of Mississippi Press, 1990.

————. *The Unfinished Quest of Richard Wright.* Tr. Isabel Barzun. 2nd ed. Urbana: University of Illinois Press, 1993.

————. *The World of Richard Wright.* Jackson: University Press of Mississippi, 1985.

Felgar, Robert. *Richard Wright.* Boston: Twayne, 1980.

Fishburn, Katherine. *Richard Wright's Hero: The Faces of a Rebel-Victim.* Metuchen, NJ: Scarecrow Press, 1977.

Gates, Henry Louis, Jr., and K. A. Appiah, ed. *Richard Wright: Critical Perspectives Past and Present.* New York: Amistad, 1993.

Gayle, Addison, Jr. *Richard Wright: Ordeal of a Native Son.* Garden City, NY: Doubleday, 1980.

Gibson, Donald B. *The Politics of Literary Expression: A Study of Major Black Writers.* Westport, CT: Greenwood Press, 1981.

————, ed. *Five Black Writers: Essays on Wright, Ellison, Baldwin, Hughes and LeRoi Jones.* New York: New York University Press, 1970.

Hellenbrand, Harold. "Bigger Thomas Reconsidered: *Native Son,* Film and *King Kong.*" *Journal of American Culture* 6 (1983): 84–95.

Holladay, Hilary. "*Native Son*'s Guilty Man." *CEA Critic* 54 (1992): 30–36.

Hynes, Joseph. "*Native Son* Fifty Years Later." *Cimarron Review* No. 102 (January 1993): 91–97.

Kinnamon, Keneth. *The Emergence of Richard Wright: A Study in Literature and Society.* Urbana: University of Illinois Press, 1972.

———. *A Richard Wright Bibliography: Fifty Years of Criticism and Commentary 1933–1982.* Westport, CT: Greenwood Press, 1988.

———, ed. *New Essays on* Native Son. Cambridge: Cambridge University Press, 1990.

Klotman, Phyllis R. "Moral Distancing as a Rhetorical Technique in *Native Son:* A Note on 'Fate.' " *CLA Journal* 18 (1974–75): 284–91.

Magistrale, Tony. "From St. Petersburg to Chicago: Wright's *Crime and Punishment.*" *Comparative Literature Studies* 23 (1986): 59–70.

Ogbaa, Kalu. "Protest and the Individual Talents of Three Black Novelists." *CLA Journal* 35 (1991–92): 159–84.

Payne, Ladell. "A Clear Case: Richard Wright 1908–1960." In Payne's *Black Novelists and the Southern Literary Tradition.* Athens: University of Georgia Press, 1981, pp. 54–79.

Pudaloff, Ross. "Celebrity as Identity: Richard Wright, *Native Son,* and Mass Culture." *Studies in American Fiction* 11 (1983): 3–18.

Reed, Kenneth T. "*Native Son:* An American *Crime and Punishment.*" *Studies in Black Literature* 1 (Summer 1970): 33–34.

Reilly, John M. "Self-Portraits by Richard Wright." *Colorado Quarterly* 20 (1971): 31–45.

Roache, Joel. " 'What Had Made Him and What He Meant': The Politics of Wholeness in 'How "Bigger" Was Born.' " *Substance* No. 15 (1976): 133–45.

Sanders, Ronald. "Relevance for the Sixties: Richard Wright Then and Now." *Negro Digest* 18 (December 1968): 83–98.

Schraufnagel, Noel. "Wright and the Protest Novel." In Schraufnagel's *From Apology to Protest: The Black American Novel.* DeLand, FL: Everett/Edwards, 1973, pp. 19–32.

Sisney, Mary F. "The Power and Horror of Whiteness: Wright and Ellison Respond to Poe." *CLA Journal* 29 (1985–86): 82–90.

Smith, Valerie. "Alienation and Creativity in the Fiction of Richard Wright." In Smith's *Self-Discovery and Authority in Afro-American Narrative*. Cambridge, MA: Harvard University Press, 1987, pp. 75–87.

Trotman, C. James, ed. *Richard Wright: Myths and Realities*. New York: Garland, 1988.

Walls, Doyle W. "The Clue Undetected in Richard Wright's *Native Son*." *American Literature* 57 (1985): 125–28.

Watson, Edward A. "Bessie's Blues." *New Letters* 38, No. 2 (Winter 1971): 64–70.

Index of
Themes and Ideas